C
Cause of the Universe
Ultimate Cause UC

Introduction to Ultimate Cause
Foundation for Complete Philosophy

By

Neil C.P. Dukelow

authorHOUSE™

1663 LIBERTY DRIVE, SUITE 200
BLOOMINGTON, INDIANA 47403
(800) 839-8640
WWW.AUTHORHOUSE.COM

First published by AuthorHouse 08/03/05

ISBN: 1-4184-9983-8 (e)
ISBN: 1-4184-9982-X (sc)
ISBN: 1-4184-9981-1 (dj)

Library of Congress Control Number: 2004096967

Printed in the United States of America
Bloomington, Indiana

This book is printed on acid-free paper.

DEDICATION

This book is dedicated to you who think about Ultimate Cause.

INDEBTED
I am indebted to everyone who touched my life. I think of you often.
When all is said and done, memories remain.

SYMBOLS
C is the symbol for cause of the universe and UC for Ultimate Cause.
U is for universe.
C = cause of the universe = UC = Ultimate Cause = cause of causes =
first cause.
U = universe. VR = virtual reality

FORWARD

My goal was to know and experience all life has to offer. I have. I know the universe and its cause. I have experienced the universe, the world, human cultures. I experience knowing another and being completely known by another. I know UC is my companion. UC completely, unconditionally knows and enjoys me without judgment. I am in UC's memory outside the universe. So are you.

Join me in thinking about Ultimate Cause. We know UC by inference from our knowledge of the universe.

You already have the idea of cause of the universe in your mind. Since the beginning of human thought, people have thought about cause of the universe by inference from their knowledge of the universe. Into their idea of cause of the universe they mixed visions, dreams, hopes, and fears and called it God. Here is a purification (demystification) of cause of the universe

You are busy. Still, you need a philosophy that logically answers the basic questions of life. You have wondered about cause of the universe. It may have been subconsciously. Bringing your subconscious thoughts about UC to conscious thought will reward you with UC's point of view, personal tranquility, and social harmony.

You owe it to yourself to take some time to orient your thinking to Ultimate Cause. When your thinking is UC-centric, all ordinary daily thought, religion, science, and philosophy are coordinated.

The government of the United States of America is based on freedom, the equality of people, separation of church and state, and natural moral laws. These come from the idea of UC, that traces back to many philosophers and Jesus' teaching.

The future of mankind depends on having Ultimate Cause as the foundation of our daily thoughts, social structures, religions, sciences, and philosophies.

From the beginning of human rationality, people have wanted to know cause of all they knew, Ultimate Cause. People were so intensely interested that they grasped at dreams, visions, revelations. Now we can logically know cause of all we know. Here it is. You can know cause of the universe for the price of the book. Have your own book to underline and annotate.

You want to know how it really is.
Start here and by the end of the book
you will know cause of the universe.
Ultimate Cause is your most intimate companion.

It makes a difference to you yourself,
your culture and the people of the world
what you think about cause of the universe.

You are your thoughts. They are all
of the mortal universe except for Ultimate Cause.

THINK
The universe is a box.
Think outside the box.
Think of cause of the box.
That is Ultimate Cause.

This book is about cause of the whole universe from galaxies of stars to subatomic particles, from DNA to human cultures.

In seeking to know, in contributing to knowing, and in knowing cause of the universe, all people, all thought, sciences, religions, and philosophies are united.

We know Ultimate Cause by inference from our knowledge of the universe as capability to cause the universe to be as it is.

With the point of view of Ultimate Cause, we see that UC likes and enjoys everything and everyone. We can too.

We work and struggle in the processes of life. It all ends. It is all mortal—except for Ultimate Cause.

The mortality and recycling of the universe make sense when we think of it as a drama for UC to experience and enjoy. Our existence, birth, and growth depend on mortality and recycling.

UC is not mortal, so is not moral, likes and enjoys everyone and everything.

Ultimate Cause is our most intimate companion, sharing our every thought and feeling. UC has it all in memory beyond the existence of the universe.

This is the capability of Ultimate Cause.

This is your opportunity to know Ultimate Cause without visions, dreams, revelations or mysteries for the price of the book.

"Every eleven-year-old should read this book." – Charlie Warren

(This is a how-to book. Have your own copy to highlight and annotate.)

TABLE OF CONTENTS

I
KNOW THE UNIVERSE

II

KNOW ULTIMATE CAUSE

B

ANSWERING QUESTIONS

B 1

ULTIMATE CAUSE IN LITERATURE

B 2

EVIL

B 3

UC AND GOD

Z

INTELLECTUAL REVOLUTION

B 4

PROOF

B 5

ON FAILURE

III
PRACTICE
KNOW YOURSELF

THINKING LIKE ULTIMATE CAUSE

SUMMARY

THOUGHTS

CHECK UP

MONK

CONCLUSION

IV
APPENDICES

APPENDIX 1
THE SEARCH FOR ULTIMATE CAUSE
APPENDIX 2
HOW TO THINK OF CAUSE OF THE UNIVERSE

APPENDIX 7

THESES AND FULFILLED HOPES

APPENDIX 8

PHILOSOPHERS

APPENDIX 9

POSTSCRIPT

APPENDIX 10

THOUGHTS

BIBLIOGRAPHY

PREFACE

Dear Reader: Welcome to thinking about cause of the universe.

I hope that knowing Ultimate Cause comes to mean as much to you as it does to me. I am logically certain of UC. UC is my closest companion, my buddy. UC knows me completely. UC knows me better than I know myself. UC knows my every thought and feeling, even my subconscious.

No matter what your circumstances, rich or poor, living in a mansion, mud or branch hut, cave or prison, UC is your companion.

In shared companionship with UC, you are companion of everyone on earth.

I hope there are enough details, repetitions, and practices so you automatically think about UC.

The reward is great. You can know UC so well that when you feel down, you laugh to UC and say, "UC, you made it this way. You are experiencing this with me. We are experiencing mortality together. How wonderful and seemingly absurd, that you, (cause of the whole universe of galaxies to subatomic particles) experience this with me. Knowing your companionship makes it all right. "

The future of mankind depends on the people whose thinking is UC-centric.

When you are consciously aware of UC, you can communicate with others about your experience with UC. You can contribute to making UC-centric thought the foundation of all thought. You can share how to think about UC.

You are free. The universe is yours with UC. As Jesus said, "You shall know the truth and the truth will set you free."

You will be glad you have your own book to highlight and annotate. You will refer to this book many times.

Sincerely,

Neil C. P. Dukelow

THINGS I WANT YOU TO KNOW ABOUT THIS BOOK

The message is real. I do experience Ultimate Cause as my companion. I do think to UC. I do think UC's response from my knowledge of the universe.   I do laugh to UC.

The story line (including the characters) is sheath that presents and illustrates how to know UC.

This is more than a book to be read. Ultimate Cause is the center to which all thought, people, philosophy, religion and science relate.

INTRODUCTION

The great need of mankind is for a common foundation for human thought that can be the base for world culture that provides as good a life as possible for every person on earth. That foundation is "cause of the universe-centric thought" that coordinates: philosophy, science, religion and ordinary everyday thoughts.

Ultimate Cause-centric thought, leads to moral culture that is compatible with the way people are. The goal is for people to live compatibly and work together to develop and to maintain social structures that make for the best possible life for everyone on earth.

Join me in building that foundation. The foundation is "cause of the universe-centric thought". It is having the viewpoint of Ultimate Cause.

The purpose of this book is to provide enough resources so you can conceptualize Ultimate Cause. It is to answer questions you may have about UC.

Children understand cause and effect. They understand presence. They know when their parents are present. It is important to children to know that they have parents. So it is important for us to know Ultimate Cause and enjoy UC's companionship.

As adults we need to distinguish between ideas that are good, right, and useful, from ideas that are not good, not right, and some even harmful to us, other people, the people of the world. We want evidence. We want ideas to be right from every angle. The idea of UC is right from every angle.

Ultimate Cause is presented from many points of view. In doing this, there is repetition. When you know UC, you will enjoy the repetition. You will enjoy thinking about UC.

Ideas about UC develop. We are constantly learning about the universe and realizing UC is enjoying it all with us.

All our thoughts, including all thoughts about science, religion, philosophy, mortality, and ordinary life, are coordinated and make sense when they are associated with Ultimate Cause of the universe.

SHORT THESES

By following the rules of cause and effect, we come to know cause of the universe by inference from our knowledge of the universe. We know Ultimate Cause in human terms, as our companion, sharing our every thought and feeling, preserving it all in memory beyond the existence of the universe. We are moral because of our mortality. We exist for UC to experience the drama of our lives, as we develop from instinctive to rational moral living. We can enjoy the drama along with UC. Religions, sciences, philosophies and every day rational thought contribute to knowing UC and in this are coordinated.

I

KNOW THE UNIVERSE

CONVERSATION 1
MY FRIEND

Sitting comfortably in our living room, I said to my friend, "You have lived many years. We are at the end of a millennium, the year 2000. You have seen most of the century, eighty years or so. I think it is more than mine. I was born in 1920. We have seen prosperity turn into depression and the Second World War. We have seen technology provide us with computers, the Internet, man walking on the moon, nanotechnology, DNA, gene therapy. We now see that the universe is expanding. It started from nothing and expanded till it is billions of galaxies, each with billions of stars. Tell me, friend, share the wisdom you have observed."

SHARE YOUR WISDOM

He responded, "You are right. Like you, I have seen many things. I have not thought about wisdom. What wisdom do I have? What is wisdom? I suppose wisdom is to know how to attain a full contented mind. Wisdom guides to an orderly society in which everyone can have the best possible life.

"We have everything a person could desire. We have abundant food, air conditioned living, health care, instant communication around the world. We have music, art, entertainment, everything for the abundant life."

He paused, and went on, "It seems to me that all knowledge is important. Certainly, many disciplines are contributing to the fullness of our lives. Consider physics, chemistry, biology, astronomy, agriculture, technology, economics, psychology, sociology, anthropology, painting,

1

music, government, business, manufacturing, architecture, education, research, laborers, clerks, technicians—. You name it. We are the recipients of the work of multitudes."

My friend paused. He looked out the window. The birds were at the feeder, eating sunflower seeds and peanuts. The squirrels were scampering through the trees. The deer occasionally come to drink at the bird bath and eat corn. Rafts of geese sail down to land on the lake. Children play on the swings and slide. People walk by with their dogs.

My friend continued. He was musing: "Yes, we have everything man can desire. Information is a flood. It seems redundant to mention electricity, running water, indoor plumbing, telephone, radio, TV, computers, satellites, satellite dishes, cable, broad band, multibillion dollar corporations, nanotechnology, the genome, gene therapy, stem cell therapy, our families and friends.

"Still, there are difficulties in the world. There are famines, wars, refugees by the millions, people starving. There are zealots that inflict misery, pain, even death for their cause."

I said, "My friend, you are absolutely right. You cause me to think of people who are not as comfortable as we are. I think of the people who live where there is civil war, where there is conflict, who are dying for lack of the necessities of life; people in pain and misery they cannot escape. I think of my friend having lost his bladder to cancer. I think of a friend with throat cancer in remission, his wife dying from cancer that eventually squeezed her lungs so she could not breathe as she was fully conscious to her last five minutes. I think of a young man who lost his legs in war. I think of the unemployed."

My friend was silent. Then he said, "You ask me to share wisdom. I ask you: What wisdom do you have to share? It seems that a person should be willing to do what one asks of others.

"How do we make sense of it? What is it all about?"

"Fair enough." I replied. And so I proceeded: "Indeed, we do have everything a person could desire. We are grateful to those around us and people in the past whose work contribute to our comfort.

"These are things of the earth, part of the universe. We are in the web of life that spreads back millions of years. We are in a struggle to survive. We struggle to survive as individual persons. But we find that we survive as groups of people. We need other people to survive. We survive as families, tribes, nations, areas of people. All the people of the world are one people. We survive together. We depend on each other. We can destroy each other. We all need to realize our commonality. There are yet people who do not feel a part of it. Humanity is fragmented. Do you agree?"

My friend said, "Certainly you are right. We are each of us and as groups in the struggle to survive. The resources of the earth are limited. Areas of the world will sustain only so many people. When there are more than the area will sustain, they have to get resources from other areas or go to another area. If the people of other areas will not provide nor allow them to move, there is conflict. Of course, this applies on the personal level also. Every person and group wants to keep what they have to insure survival.

"Then there is the matter of personal pain and suffering in the natural processes of life. You have mentioned some of them from personal experience. Everyone has such stories. Everyone faces the possibilities. No one is immune from mortality. Everyone faces the possibility of disease, pain. We all die."

My friend paused and continued, "You know, I think of times I have been utterly miserable, cold, wet, hungry, lost, in the dark, lonely to despair. I had no thoughts but for light, shelter, warmth, food, home, familiar territory, comfortable surroundings, friends. Everything else was out of my mind. I was in utter despair.

"Is there wisdom about personal discouragement, pain, suffering, disease, death, despair, fear, frustration, rage? Is there wisdom about personal mental anguish? Is there wisdom about how one handles one's situation and what happens to one? Is there wisdom about the social situations that lead to anguish, to frantic rage? Some people are in a state of rage when they compare their situation to that of others."

I said, "Your analysis is right. People need an answer to the questions of life. How can I feel at home in this world? Why does the universe exist? Why does mankind exist? Why do I exist? Why am I here? Why are things as they are? Why diseases? Why suffering and pain? Why the conflict among people? Why despair, rage?

"What are we to do? How can we escape mental anguish? How can we solve the social disparities? What can be done about organized aggression, nations seeking dominion over others? What can we do about leaders, powerful people, dictators, mistreating their own people and seeking to dominate other people and nations? What can we do about terrorism? What can we do about ideologies that teach to kill those who disagree?

"There is need for personal peace of mind, contentment, tranquility, feeling of being in harmony within oneself, with people of other cultures, with the whole of mankind. There is need for understanding. We need to understand why we are here on earth and what we are to do. There is need for personal tranquility. There is also need for social harmony. There is need for something to bring people together, realize we need each other. Everyone needs a satisfying place in the socioeconomic systems of the world.

"There is need for personal satisfaction. When people are satisfied within themselves, when they have a complete philosophy, they will seek harmony with all other people. Some people attain tranquility even in severe pain, misery, and suffering."

My friend said, "You are right. We agree. Many agree with the analysis. There is need for personal tranquility and social harmony. How do we attain it? What is the solution? Is there a solution?"

MORALITY AND ETHICS

I said, "There is little we can do about some of the processes of the earth such as earthquakes, landslides, floods, hurricanes, droughts, growing old, weakening, and inevitable death. We do what we can to prevent and alleviate suffering. These are our moral and ethical responsibilities.

"We need to accept that we are part of the processes, part of mortality. We need to do what we can to make life as comfortable and long as we can. We need to accept our mortality and our moral responsibility. We need a philosophy that accepts our mortality and guides us in morality."

THE PROBLEMS
PERSONAL TRANQUILITY AND SOCIAL HARMONY

My friend said, "There seem to be two problems. One is the problem of personal tranquility. It may also be termed the problem of frustration, despair, envy, anger, rage. How do we have a prevailing mood of tranquility? The other problem is how do we attain social harmony? It seems to me that personal tranquility will produce social harmony. Is there a solution to these problems?"

THE SOLUTION

I said, "I think there is. The solution is in the minds of the people of the world. The solution is in everyone knowing Ultimate Cause.

"When we know UC, we know the purpose of living. The purpose of our being is so UC can experience with each of us our unique lives. UC is our companion. This brings personal tranquility. Knowing UC brings social harmony. UC values and enjoys each person. We too are to like and enjoy everyone. We learn to enjoy others as we realize UC already enjoys them.

"Those who know UC have a view of the universe that makes sense. They have a cosmic view that joins all the ideas of religion, science, and philosophy into one understanding.

"Religions satisfy our needs for community, arts, poetry, music, ritual, imagination, hope—. The sciences keep us searching for knowledge. The more we know about the universe, the better we know Ultimate Cause. The more we know, the better we can organize our social structures to make life as good as possible for everyone.

"When all is said and done, we have had experiences. What is left is memories. When we no longer live, those memories remain in Ultimate Cause."

HOW TO KNOW ULTIMATE CAUSE

I continued, "As I think about how I came to know Ultimate Cause, I notice that I made some decisions that enabled me to know UC. Without these decisions, I would not know UC. I would not think in terms of UC. I think everyone needs to make these decisions. Here are my decisions.

"I accept that the universe is rational. There is cause for every phenomenon. The universe is processes. I accept objective thinking for myself and Ultimate Cause. I accept Ultimate Cause is abstract, outside the universe. I think of UC as capability to cause the universe to be as it is. I infer Ultimate Cause from my knowledge of the universe.

"If I am uncertain about these, I am uncertain about Ultimate Cause. Then I miss the benefits of knowing Ultimate Cause. I miss the personal tranquility and social harmony that comes from knowing Ultimate Cause. I miss knowing UC is my companion."

My friend looked at me in wonderment. Finally, he said, "You think people are capable of this? Everyone can accept: rationality, cause and effect relationships extended to cause of the universe, the whole universe is in process? Everyone can think objectively? Everyone can think of the abstract? Everyone can infer Ultimate Cause from the phenomena of the universe? You are saying that everyone needs to have a complete philosophy. Everyone can accept rationality, cause and effect, processes, objectivity and think of the abstract. And these are the basis for knowing C. Why, I don't know anyone else who has even thought of these things!"

"Yes," I said, "it seems like a big order. But many problems are solved when we have UC as the base of our philosophies. We know why the universe exists and why we are here. We have personal tranquility and social harmony. We enjoy everything about the world and people as UC does.

"I think people are aware of Ultimate Cause, at least subconsciously. We need to think and talk about UC. Many of our difficulties are because we do not have the perspective of Ultimate Cause.

"Some people have not heard of the idea of UC. Others may have ignored UC because of skepticism about rationality, cause and effect, processes, objectivity, and the abstract. Ask yourself if you accept them. Do you accept rationality, cause and effect, processes, objectivity, and abstract to include Ultimate Cause? If you do, you know or can know UC. Let's consider each point one at a time."

RATIONAL

"I think most everyone is rational and considers the universe to be rational. Rational means understandable, logical. There are two parts to the rationality of the universe. One is the rationality of the universe itself. Is it understandable, logical? The second is our own rationality. Am I rational? Are you rational? Do we think logically?

"Yes, I consider myself rational. I consider you and everyone rational. There is a reason for our thoughts, speech, and actions. We think rationally with our knowledge and thinking skills. We may seem irrational to others, but with the hierarchy of our thoughts, we are logical to ourselves. I would not be one to deny my own or your rationality.

"As for the rationality of the universe, I would not be one to try to show rationally that the universe is not rational."

My friend said, "All right. We don't know everything about the universe. We never will know everything. You say we should keep working on it. Encourage experimentation. Encourage everyone to keep seeking new knowledge. I agree. You also say we know enough about the universe to know Ultimate Cause by inference. I accept that the universe is rational. I accept my own and your rationality. I think everyone is rational within their knowledge and thinking skills."

CAUSE AND EFFECT

After a pause, he said, "You say we need to accept that for every phenomenon, there is some cause. We keep looking till we find adequate cause for every phenomenon."

"Yes," I said, "it is natural for us to look for the cause of things. Cause and effect is involved in everything we do. Everything is part of long strings of cause and effect. For every phenomenon, there is a cause or causes. Our experience of cause and effect is so strong that we automatically look for the cause of every phenomenon. When we are sick, we look for the cause.

"I accept that everything in the universe has a cause. When I know enough, I can know that cause. When I go back following the trail of cause, I come to the universe itself. I want to know all I can about cause of the universe. For convenience, I give cause of the universe a symbol C. Cause of the universe is adequate to cause everything about the universe."

My friend said, "I have no problem with cause and effect. I have heard people say that the universe just is. Some say the universe has always been as it is. Some say the universe was created as it is without processes of development. Some say it has no cause."

I responded, "I know. You are right. Those ideas exist. To me, denying cause of the universe is denying our experience. It is logical to explore the universe and infer what we can about its cause.

"There is much to be discovered. Yet, I think we know enough about the universe to infer some things about its cause. And certainly we want to keep on exploring and learning."

PROCESSES

My friend said, "You say we need to think that the universe is in process."

I said, "Yes. It means we are also in process. We are learning. We are developing new knowledge and thinking skills. We are developing complexity and intelligence as UC intends. This is important because we think the universe is static till we learn it is dynamic, changing, processes. We think the universe is static because from infancy, we program our minds to think of things as they are. Our education emphasizes memory. Processes need to be taught as part of things as they are.

"The discovery of the red shift in the spectrum of galaxies shows the universe is expanding. This indicates the universe had a start, is developing. The universe is a continual process, is constantly changing. Recycling is a continual process.

"As indication of the change that came in people's thinking in the last century, consider some examples. It has been reported that Einstein in his early years thought it repugnant to think that the universe had not existed. This view was common.

"Another example is that people are gradually being convinced that natural resources are limited. The fish of the sea and the trees of the forest need to be replenished by processes. We are using oil and coal as though there is no end.

"My father was strong for conservation. He was for preserving wildlife habitat. Yet when I mentioned that the sea was being polluted, his immediate comment was, 'No. The sea is big.'

"It is still difficult to convince people that we need to conserve natural resources. We are using up the natural resources and polluting our environment. It seems as though people think God will providentially create gas and oil when we use them up. God will replenish the land. God will put more fish in the sea. God will provide. We seem to think that natural resources are not our responsibility.

"We are not above the processes of the earth. Creatures cease to live when they don't adjust to the natural processes. We need to take responsibility for our environment and natural resources. They developed in processes over millions of years. Population is limited by resources. Natural processes limit population. Human population will be controlled by natural processes of starvation, disease, and conflict unless we rationally control it.

"Part of the drama for UC is man developing skills, knowledge, and cultures. The drama is in our developing mental tools such as the scientific method, mathematics, logic—. It is in developing knowledge of the universe, such as of electricity, genome, DNA, viruses, galaxies, the red shift, models of atoms—. It is in our developing tools such as telephones, TV, automobiles, airplanes, computers, jet engines, atomic reactors—.

"The drama is in our developing empathy for our fellow man, the developing of philosophy, religions, knowledge of UC, cultures, governments, socioeconomic systems that include everyone, with the goal of everyone on earth having the best possible life.

"I look at a baby and think, 'By the instructions in a single cell, that baby has developed and will grow up to be and do all that a person is and does. Each of us started from our own single cell with all the instructions for a complete human being. This is not an occasional occurrence but billions of people and all the animals develop by the instructions in their own original single cell. The whole universe and life is in process, changing, evolving, recycling.'"

OBJECTIVITY

My friend said, "You mentioned objectivity. I presume you mean we are to think objectively. We are to see things just as they are, themselves alone."

I said, "Yes. Seeing things objectively is seeing them as they are. Thinking of things objectively is keeping ourselves out of the picture. When I consider something objectively I see it independent of myself. I sort of stand off and look at it, as it is itself, independent of anything else. We think of C separate from the universe. We think of C independent of the universe. We think of C separate from ourselves. C sees us objectively. C sees us as entities in ourselves.

"We also look at ourselves objectively. We sort of stand off and look at ourselves. This is seeing ourselves as C does. When we see ourselves objectively, we see that we are part of the universe, part of the processes. Thinking of ourselves objectively helps us escape our ego. It enables us to accept our mortality. It enables us to accept that we are entirely dependent on C. We see ourselves as part of the drama of the universe. We think of ourselves in C's memory. We think of our responsibility for morality and ethics.

"We need to think objectively about ourselves and C."

ABSTRACT

My friend said, "You say C is abstract. I presume you mean that C is not the universe nor part of the universe. C is not the material or the energy of the universe. C is not the natural laws. Can you make clearer the idea that C is abstract?"

I said, "You are right. We think of UC outside the box of the universe. C is not the universe nor part of it. C is separate from the material, energy, natural laws of the universe. C is beyond the universe, outside the universe. C is not a phenomenon of the universe. C is not a 'being.' C is not 'a,' not 'the,' not 'he,' not 'she,' not 'it,' not 'infinite,' not 'living,' not 'is,' not anything we know of as part of the universe. C had everything about the universe designed, so it is a continuing process of development. C is beyond infinity. C designed and made infinity. C designed and made the universe so there is space and time.

"Space is what is between objects. Space is that which things occupy. Time is duration of phenomena. Time and space exist as measures of relative conditions and positions of the material and energy of the universe."

(Defining space and time this way does not preclude research considering time and space as entities in themselves. Ideas about UC should not be used to limit thinking, research, the making of equations and models. Ultimate Cause is known by inference from what we know about the universe. Ideas about UC are not to be used to limit learning more about the universe from which we infer Ultimate Cause. Knowing the universe and inferring more about UC is a continuing process.)

"We are using abstractions all the time. We start our formal education learning to use abstract letters and numbers. We learn to disconnect them from things. We learn to think of them as independent entities in themselves. Words themselves are abstract. We start out with A is for apple and 3 is for three oranges. Then we abstract the letters and numbers."

My friend said, "Well. There seem to be degrees of abstract. There are abstractions like letters and numbers and then there is C."

"Yes," I said, "we need to be careful when we talk about Ultimate Cause. We can only conceptualize UC in terms of our human experience. UC is not anything of the universe. Yet UC, having caused the universe, has everything about the universe as concept in what to us is mind. In that way the universe is virtual reality to C.

"UC, in what to us would be something like mind, has all human possibilities of thought, feeling and action. UC has all the capability of the tools we make such as computers, sensors, memory instruments—. UC built all our possibilities and capabilities of the instruments we make into the universe. UC knows us, causes us to be as we are.

"So Ultimate Cause is that abstract that thought of a universe, designed it; made it continuing processes. UC is everywhere present in that UC is aware of everything. C enjoys and remembers all about the universe including every person's thoughts and feelings. UC has all our capabilities and more. We are not saying UC has a physical brain to contain memory or chemical emotions. We can describe and think of UC only in our terms and in terms of our experiences. UC experiences with us exactly as we do and more.

"We practice thinking about the abstract as we think about Santa Claus, the Easter Bunny, fairies— They prepare out minds for thinking about the abstract.

"When I was substituting in the Bonner Springs Schools, I told the story about Little Red Riding Hood Buffalo. One of the children turned to a classmate wondering what this was about. He was not acquainted with the childhood stories that prepare our minds to think of the abstract."

THE CAPABILITY OF ULTIMATE CAUSE

After a pause—it was quite some time—we were reflecting. My friend said, "I have been thinking about how I view the earth. As I look out at the earth, it is so solid. It is so big and stable. It just is. I just accept it and think no more about it. Then sometimes I think of the earth as a big ball suspended in space and wonder, what is this earth all about? How did this come to be? There are continents, vast oceans. I am impressed when out on a ship. They say the ocean is miles deep. I look at the sky, the clouds, the rain. I think of the snowstorms in winter. I look at the sky with the stars moving around at night and the sun and moon. It is all so solid and permanent, I say to myself, 'It just is.' Then I think. 'There must be some cause.'

"You are saying we can think about and know cause of the universe. You are saying that C would have the capabilities that are built into the universe and more. C has the capabilities of the people and tools people make.

"An eggs has the compressed instructions for the development of a complete person. We are capable of being aware of many things and have tools to be aware and remember. C has all these capabilities and more. So we cannot limit UC's ability to have compressed memory and compress instructions.

"You are saying that knowing this, we know UC knows our every thought and feeling. So we can think to and laugh to UC about our mortality. And we can think UC's response from our knowledge of the universe.

"You say we can know UC so well that we laugh to UC about our situation. I guess I will have to incorporate the idea of UC more into my thinking to do that."

SUMMARY

I said, "Now to summarize. We accept: the rationality of the universe and our own rationality. For every phenomenon, there is cause. The universe is a phenomenon so has cause, C. The universe is processes. C made the processes of the universe. We are part of the processes. We can think objectively. We can conceptualize C separate from the universe. C sees us objectively. We can think of ourselves objectively. We can think of the abstract. We think about C as abstract but associated with the universe. We think of C causing the universe. Since things do not cause themselves, cause of the universe is not the universe nor part of it. Cause of the universe is objective to the universe. C is separate from the universe, but associated with the universe as its cause. UC is aware of everything that happens in the universe and has everything in memory beyond the existence of the universe".

CONVERSATION 2
T

There was a knock on the door and T came in. He said, "I caught you guys talking without me. You look like you have been having a session. Fill me in. You can't get away without me."

I said, "Sure. We are glad to have you. We have been serious. Let me fill you in." So I briefly told him the story of our conversation. Of course, he had his response ready. He always did.

He swung into high gear with the frankness he always showed, "There you go again. What you propose is ridiculous, impossible. No one believes that stuff. It will never fly. You say the universe is rational. No one understands the universe. They think they do. People are not rational. Look at all the stuff they believe. Thinking something does not make it so. As for cause and effect, we never know the cause of anything completely. Instead of an outside cause of the universe, I think no cause is needed. If the universe has a cause, it is internal combustion. There is enough stuff around to be the cause. As for processes, God made it as it is right now. There are changes and growth, not processes. God put those fossils in the rocks. As for objectivity, I am subjective. I am concerned with the things that affect me and humanity. Forget objectivity.

"As for abstract, there is nothing separate from the universe. The universe just goes on and on as the astronomers tell us. Even Einstein is reported to have said it was repugnant to him to think of the universe not being. As for C or UC as you call it... pure imagination. I would rather have God and revelations."

T paused, and then said, "How is that for a demolition derby! I am serious. This is whole rubbish. People have tried it in the past and failed. The records indicate they thought about it but couldn't do it."

I said, "I love you, I love you, I love you, T. You always cut to the chase. You are wonderful, wonderful, wonderful, T. You have rejected rationality. You deny cause-and-effect relationships. You deny objectivity. You deny the universe is processes. You consider abstractions rubbish. Of course you do this as a challenge. You live like everyone else. You are rational. You use cause and effect. You think objectively as much as anyone. You use processes. You use abstract thinking all the time."

T responded, "Of course a person does not have to be a dolt to reject your idea of UC. I just don't see it. Of course I recognize that nothing can be proven. So-called proofs are matters of consistency. And we consider things are proven when they work. We prove usefulness. We cannot get outside the universe to look at it objectively. We don't have references outside the universe to prove it. We are stuck in the universe and cannot get outside of the universe to look at it. We can't get outside of ourselves to think in other than human terms."

I said, "T what would it take for you to take the idea of UC seriously? What is your thinking?"

T AND RATIONALITY

T responded, "Let's take the parts one at a time. Consider your first point, that the universe is rational. There is so much that doesn't make sense to me. Look at the people of the world. The news is full of floods, earthquakes, fires, famines, diseases, people starving, people suffering in pain, poverty, wars, people killing others, revolutions, terrorism. There is so much inhumanity of man-to-man. There is so much senseless killing, conflict. It just doesn't make sense."

I said, "T, I hear you saying that you want to understand why things are as they are. You want to know what you can do to make things better. You are asking for rationality. You want everything to make sense.

"Knowing Ultimate Cause is the answer to your questions. Rationally we go to the cause of things. So we go to the cause of the universe.

"We make things either because we need them to continue our mortal existence or we make things to enjoy them.

"Cause of the universe, not being mortal, does not need anything of the universe to survive. So (in human terms) Ultimate Cause caused the universe to experience and enjoys it. UC enjoys observing mankind developing knowledge, understanding, skills, cultures—. UC experiences us, something like we experience a drama. UC enjoys watching us write the script as we develop from living by instinct to rational self-conscious moral living.

"It makes sense for a finite earth and limited universe to be mortal and recycling. It makes sense for us to be part of the mortal and recycling processes. The world makes sense when we think of Ultimate Cause making the universe to experience and enjoy it. It makes sense for the finite earth to be mortal, to be dynamic, and be in the processes of recycling. We are part of this dynamic, mortal, recycling earth."

T thought for a while and said, "Well. You say it makes sense when one knows Ultimate Cause. Knowing UC is the key to knowing why things are as they are, including the miseries of mankind. There is a logical reason that makes sense. Ultimate Cause caused the universe to experience and enjoy. I will have to consider the rest of the ideas about C to see where rationality fits. Let's go on."

T AND CAUSE AND EFFECT

T said, "Your next point is cause and effect. There is cause for every phenomenon. I rely on cause and effect. The scientific method is based on finding cause-and-effect relationships.

"You are saying that the whole universe, including ourselves, is a phenomenon. We infer the properties of its cause. You call the cause of the universe Ultimate Cause because cause of the universe is not a phenomenon for which we can seek cause. We can't investigate C directly. There can be no inferred cause for C.

"I understand you are saying that we can use our own experiences of making things as illustrations of what C would have experienced creating the universe. You are saying that C would want the universe. C would have the universe designed and made with ongoing processes. The universe would be as C wants it. So, C likes the universe. In our terms, C enjoys the universe as we enjoy things we make.

"I see what you are doing.

"The universe is a lot of systems and processes. C is not limited as we are. We can give our attention and be aware of one or a few things at a time. C is aware of everything in the universe, every subatomic particle, and all the time. C has memory better than we do. UC remembers everything. You are saying that to make sense of the universe, look at it as a drama for UC to enjoy."

I said, "Whoa, T. You have grasped what I have been saying perfectly. UC experiences with every person his or her unique life. UC experiences with us our every thought and feeling. C has each of us in memory, our whole lives. C has us in memory, beyond the existence of the universe."

T said, "I have analyzed cause and effect. I need to think about it some more. There are people who say the universe just is, and there is no cause. Let's go on to your next point."

T AND PROCESS

T said, "Your next point is processes. I haven't thought much about processes. Let's think about it. You say that the universe is processes. Everything is in process. That means everything is changing. Things aren't as they were. There was a start of everything."

T reflected for a moment, not long. T has a quick mind. "As I think about it, I realize I think of things being permanent, static. The sun comes up regularly. We rely on the seasons coming regularly. People are born, live, work, grow old, and die. The earth and heavens are permanent. With slight rhythm variations, the universe seems static.

"But then you brought up the idea of an expanding universe based on the idea of galaxies of stars and the red shift indicating the galaxies are moving apart. There is the idea that the universe had a beginning. So we have the idea that the universe was started by UC from nothing, then a pinpoint. It developed into galaxies, stars, our planet—. It is continuing to develop.

"I see what you are talking about. Back of the universe is something like intelligence, capability, to cause the universe. You use the designation Ultimate Cause. UC caused the instructions of the universe so the universe develops automatically. The instructions are (in our present terminology) something like natural laws. Perhaps, the instructions are something like DNA yet to be discovered.

"The mechanisms of the universe will progressively be discovered by people who have the capability, resources and freedom to do the research and to develop the language (mathematics, vocabulary and syntax) necessary to make models for the research.

"Discovering the mechanisms of the universe may be likened to the discovery of how to make computers. What is it that instructs bits of information to relate to others to result in programs and operating machines?

"You are saying that the instructions for the universe include instructions for the processes of the earth such as rain, evaporation, plant growth, recycling of materials through plant growth, death, decay, and reuse of materials in new plants. The same processes are true of animals. Both grazers and predators eat, grow, die, and decay. The materials of their bodies are recycled through predators, scavengers, molds, insects, bacteria, plants. You are saying all these are ongoing processes. It was all designed and made (in long lines of causes and effects) by C. C wants everything as it is. We are to accept life as it comes. We are part of the processes. We are not only part of the physical processes. We are part of the intellectual processes that go back to the beginning of human thought. Every generation builds on the ideas of the past. We pass our ideas on to the next generation. This has been going on since the beginning of human thought.

"C is delighted with our research and discoveries of DNA, RNA, stem cell research and discoveries. They are part of the drama.

"C made the world a stage. We play our part. When our part is done, C has us in memory beyond the existence of the universe. You say thoughts of this give you great satisfaction."

I said, "Yes. Thinking about C completes my philosophy. My ideas have a focus. I know what life is about. As I am approaching the inevitable end of my days on earth, I think of C as my companion. As I see the wonderful things around me, I think, 'Someday I will not see them anymore. But my buddy C will. C will still be enjoying them as C has since the universe began.' I smile to myself as I walk along thinking of C enjoying with me. C will continue when I am no longer alive. Are we ready to take up objectivity?"

T said, "Oh, go ahead, I can guess what you are going to say. But I could say it better." While I was gathering my thoughts, T went on.

T AND OBJECTIVITY

T said, "I am not one to think objectively. I am concerned about people. My time and energy are consumed with my work and helping people. I think subjectively. I think of how things affect me so I know how they affect others. I think there is too much objective thinking. I take things personally. I think of how things affect me and other people."

I said, "I always admire your subjective approach. You include others in your subjectivity. I appreciate your anguish over the plight of many people in our world. You have great empathy. Also in helping people, you are good at looking at the objective hard facts of what it takes to be of help.

"I think of objectivity as thinking of things separate from everything else. I consider C alone, independent of the universe. C does not need the universe. C was before the universe existed. C will exist when the universe is no more.

"T, you know about the expanding universe. You know about the start of the universe and there must be cause. From our perspective, it must have been caused. We view C as separate from the universe. However, we know C only in terms of relationship to the universe. We need to look at ourselves objectively and UC objectively."

T said, "Of course. I see that C is separate from the universe. C has to be separate to bring energy, matter, the laws of nature, processes into being. I see that C considers us objectively as created creatures. But even objectivity can involve liking and enjoying. We have emotions and hormones."

I said, "Of course we are living normal lives as human beings in this world. We live in the culture of our time and place. I am not saying we are to give up subjective thinking. We have both subjective and objective thinking. But we need to think objectively to know UC."

T AND THE ABSTRACT

T said, "Let's go on to the abstract. I am not one to think about the abstract. I am concerned with the real, the universe, especially our human life."

I said, "T, you use abstract all the time. Numbers and letters of the alphabet are abstract. You thought of the abstract when told fairy stories, about the wee ones, grenches, goblins, angels, Santa Claus, the Easter Bunny. Children today recognize TV characters in the realm of imagination, abstract thinking. Even words are abstract."

T said, "Yeah, I knew early on what that stuff was. I can think of the abstract as well as anyone. I will have to agree there is an appeal to your idea of UC. I agree that cause of the universe is ultimate, because C is not a phenomenon which we can investigate. C is abstract and objective."

T went on, "You talk about our being limited to thinking in human terms and understanding in terms of our human experiences. You also talk about thinking about the abstract. Now tell me, how am I to think about C? Some want to think of C as a person. And you use C and UC like nicknames for a companion. And you talk about C being your buddy. These are personal terms, indicating something like a personal relationship. How can there be a personal relationship without a person?"

I said, "T, I love you. I love you. You get to the heart of things. Indeed, I do have a very frank and personal relationship to C. C knows my every thought and feeling. C knows my rationalizations. Nothing about my thoughts is hidden from C. C designed everything about me. C likes me, enjoys me. Of course, this is in our terms. C is the designer and maker of the whole universe that we know from our astronomy, physics, biology, psychology, sociology, all the sciences, and our experience. C designed us to develop the scientific method and all our discoveries. C designed us to explore the universe. C designed us so we might have God and gods.

"Now, of course, we know just a little bit about the universe, even about ourselves. But UC knows all about the universe, including us. I know that C knows all about me. C knows all about every person. I cannot hide anything from C, so why not recognize familiarity? I know that C knows my thoughts. So I talk to C by directing my thoughts to C. It is like an e-mail. C responds in my thoughts. I don't know which of my thoughts are directly from C, if any."

[C knows all about my writing this. I think C wants me to write these things. I do not know who will read them. I do not know what effect they will have, if any. Some of my experiences have come out of the blue. They make me think that C is directing events for me. Some coincidences seem impossible. You probably have had such coincidences. Of course, everything that is and that happens, C made the processes so it is as it is. Probably I am just part of the development of thought through the generations. It is my part to write this at this time. To me, it seems strange that no one has written about UC like this before. Because it seems obvious to me that multitudes of people must be thinking about Ultimate Cause.]

"I often think when I see things happening in the world, 'C designed it to be that way.' No matter how bad it seems to me, this is C's world and universe. We are all C's people.

"Yes, I think of C as a person. But all the time, I remember that C is more than any person. After all, C designed and caused the automatic continuing development of the entire universe of galaxies, our earth, and all the people. C knows all about everything. Since C knows everything about me, there is no reason for me not to be on a personal basis with C, though I know little about C, and that by inference.

"Well, I guess this is true of every relationship. You are my friend, but not limited to being my friend. You have a life I don't know about, probably that no one but UC knows about. You know and do things I don't know about. You have abilities I don't know about. You have thoughts only you and UC know about. You are greater than I know. I know you in terms of my own experience. I think you experience something like I do. That is true about my knowledge of C. I know very little about C and that only by inference. I know C in terms of my experience. C knows all about me. Nothing about me is hidden from C.

"I think of C giving me complete attention. C is able to give full attention to every person on earth and more. Full attention means knowing all there is to know. C knows all about me, you, and everyone.

"It is said that to know that you are really known and appreciated for what you are, gives the highest meaning to life. Knowing UC knows you completely, likes and enjoys you unconditionally, gives meaning to your life."

T said, "One more thing. I wonder... How? Is there any way to think of C? You know. Are there thoughts that help you?"

I said, "Yes there certainly are. In the background of my mind is a compression of all the things I know about the universe from galaxies to subatomic particles, natural laws, cosmic rays, energy; from DNA to complex human society. Also, I have a compression of C's capabilities and what C has done and is doing. I think of C conceptualizing a universe, wanting a universe, designing it, making all the rules, making the universe with all its processes of development and recycling. I think of C knowing, liking, enjoying everything about it. I think of all of it and myself in C's memory. With all of this in my mind, I think of C in human terms. I think of C as the greatest person I can imagine, the most knowledgeable, most powerful. Then, I transform, or abstract, this great person into thought, ideas, virtual reality. I take away all the things of the universe except ideas, thought. C is something like our ideas, virtual reality, thought.

"Then I think of C as a presence, an influence, like one might think of an abstraction like the United States or any other country or a corporation, an organization. These are abstractions with some similarities to C. I sometimes think of C as the CEO, although not physically present, maintaining the organization by influence. I think C is cause of the ongoing processes of the universe. C is present like the law is present, as power is present, like a parent is present as an influence wherever one is. C is an influence to be considered.

"T, what do you think?"

T scratched his head. He thought about it. Then he said, "Well, I need to think about it. This is new to me. If you can do it, I certainly can. You have practiced this. You like to think in these terms. I don't know if I can or if I want to."

I said, "T you are right. Everyone has to make up his or her own mind. I have talked to people who like these ideas and indicate they think along these lines. I have talked to people who dislike them. Ideas live in our minds or they don't. Ultimate Cause will be an integral part of your thinking or it won't"

T said, "It isn't that I think you are wrong. I have not thought in these terms. I don't know how they coordinate with my lifetime of thought. My mind is filled with my work and family."

I said, "Thank you T. You are always open to ideas. For one thing, look at the world and universe objectively. Accept it as it is. UC made it, to be, as it is. Sometimes I see things I don't like. Then I remember to think, 'C made it so it would be this way. C likes it. I can enjoy it too.' I can think something like C does."

T AND CONCLUDING THOUGHTS

As we sat together, comfortably watching the stream running from a recent rain, a northern flicker with his red crest took some peanuts, flew away, flashing the yellow feathers under his wings. A blue jay took some too. A sparrow pecked some sunflower seeds. Cars were going by.

I said, "T you are younger than we are. We have lived through most of the last century. Great discoveries have been made in our lifetime. It is hard to realize in our lifetime it was discovered that our Milky Way system is a galaxy of stars. It was discovered that the universe is made up of billions of other galaxies. It was discovered that light from the galaxies has the red shift. This indicates they are receding. The universe is expanding. This indicates that the universe had a start. These ideas did not come about without intense scrutiny. The discoveries were questioned and verified.

"In the 1920s, there was intense discussion about there being galaxies and the red shift. These were new ideas. They were new ideas to the professionals. These led to a change in the way people viewed the heavens and the earth. We saw that there is a universe out there. And our sun and earth are just part of the universe. People formerly had no reason for thinking of the heavens and earth other than just as they saw them. The stars were just points of light, except for sun, moon and planets. People talked in terms of heaven and earth. They thought of the heavens and earth as static, just being. It always had been that way and always would be. Billions was a concept without an agreed-upon definition, as was trillion. I remember the papers reporting discussions about how many zeros were on a billion and a trillion. Some in Great Britain had it different from people in the United States.

"Before the discovery of galaxies and the expanding universe, people considered the universe as being static. It always had been and would always be as it is. It was created complete as it is in a few days. Heaven was considered a place up there where people lived. Some people today have not heard about the galaxies, the red shift, the expanding universe, the beginning of the universe, Ultimate Cause."

T said, "Well, I have to admit, I have heard little about the red shift. I have never thought about it or galaxies. My attention is on my living. Why should I think about Ultimate Cause?"

I said, "There are two basic reasons for thinking about Ultimate Cause and having UC as the foundation of one's philosophy. One is personal tranquility. Knowing UC answers the personal questions about the meaning of life. We live so C can enjoy our unique experiences. The other is social harmony. We are united when we realize we are all the same to UC. C enjoys us all, regardless of who we are and what we do. C enjoys everyone. UC enjoys everyone equally, completely. So should we.

"In our companionship with UC, we are companions with each other. I am companion of everyone on earth in my companionship with UC. We are all companions in our companionship with UC. When all is said and done, the final importance of our lives is that we are important to C. Finally, we are in C's memory."

T said, "I have thought with you about UC. I understand. It makes sense logically. I suppose you can say we know UC beyond a reasonable doubt. But I haven't incorporated the idea of UC into my thinking, into my philosophy. I don't know if I can, if I will, or even if I want to. I don't know if I will ever think of UC again."

I said, "Thank you, T. All one can do is give consideration to an idea. You have done that and more. You understand UC. I suspect you will never forget Ultimate Cause. You will think about C from time to time. The idea of UC will live in your mind. I think UC lives in everyone's mind."

MY STORY

HOW I CAME TO THINK ABOUT UC

There was a considerable silence. We began to talk about what we were doing. T told about his latest project. He was describing the difficulties of people around the world. Local customs make life hard for some people. The dowry custom in parts of India and the despair of widows, child bride customs in parts of Africa where the little girls married early are unable to deliver babies, ruin their genital area and without surgical help, die ostracized in stench they can do nothing about. Stoning of girls for what is called dishonoring the family, for as little as talking to a man. Homophobia and racism that leads to murder in the United States. Conflict of Christians among themselves in Ireland. Conflict of Jews and Palestinians. Slavery of many kinds around the world. This brought silence.

My friend broke the reflections over what had transpired. He said, "I have been wondering how you came upon the idea of Ultimate Cause. There must be a story back of it."

I said, "There is quite a story. It is the story of a lifetime. But if you wish to hear part of it, I will try to tell it."

I suppose like you and everyone, the story starts early in life. It starts with my first being aware of the house where we lived, the farm, the land, my parents, my siblings, the horses, cows, chickens, ducks, geese, pigs, the activities in the kitchen, the barn, the schoolhouse, sitting in the classroom, recess, games, the church with singing and sermons, Sunday school classes, the wild creatures: rabbits, coyotes, skunks, badgers, civet cats, possums, squirrels, rafts of geese flying over, crows, all kinds of birds.

I remember evenings in the barnyard. The small children would be sitting on Stringsie, our pony. We were looking at the moon and stars, the planets. We talked about the moon and planets suspended in space, like our earth, great big balls of rock and dirt, the stars balls of fire. Natural laws, gravity, centrifugal and centripetal forces at work keeping everything in balance.

As time went on, the explanation was made that it was created by God. No one knew what God was. God is a spirit, I was told. But spirits were people after they were dead. At Halloween, we dealt with spirits.

I remember one spring playing in the lilac bushes with my tractors and trucks, watching the shadows of the leaves change by an eclipse. Two days in a row, it happened. I said to myself, 'I will remember this and look it up sometime so I can know how old I was.' Recently, I asked the librarian at Park University when that would have been. She looked it up and found that such an eclipse of the sun occurred June 9 and 10, 1926. I was five years old, would be six on August 3.

I have two memories of my sister, born when I was thirteen months old. One was when she could not yet walk. We were in the barn. Someone had told me to take care of her. I remember thinking it was not good to be sitting on the barn floor. I was about two years old. The other time was when I insisted I wanted to walk around the farm. I was about three years old. Mother was busy. So to get us out of her hair for a while, she consented. My older sister helped make some sandwiches for us to take. We started out and got about ten yards. The stickers and heat stopped us. We retreated to the house. It was a short reprieve for mother, but it wore us out.

Special ability is not needed to know Ultimate Cause. Everyone observes cause and effect. When we follow cause-and-effect relationships, we come to the cause of the whole universe.

I remember playing on the floor while my mother was ironing. I asked questions. When she answered, I kept asking "Why?"

My inquisitiveness was never stifled. Quite naturally I asked, *why the universe?* As time went on, I read St. Augustine's writing about "First Cause" creating the universe out of nothing, not complete but developing. I read Thomas Jefferson's writing about "ultimate cause." I read Erasmus Darwin's writing about "cause of causes." I read about the red shift of lines on the spectrum of light coming from receding objects. I read about the discovery that the universe is made up of galaxies of stars, and light from those galaxies has the red shift. The universe is expanding.

Things do not cause themselves. There was a "before the universe." So there was cause of the universe. Cause of the universe was before the universe, so not part of the universe.

I wondered, "What can we know about cause of the universe?"

I noticed the common way of knowing the cause of a phenomenon is to infer its cause from knowledge of the phenomenon. New planets have been discovered when it was noticed that the orbits of known planets were not what they should be from known influences. Calculations were made as to what would cause the unexpected orbits. A planet in a certain position was inferred. They looked and found it. So they found Pluto (Feb. 18, 1930). Neptune was identified in 1846.

Consequently, I sought to know cause of the universe by inference from our knowledge of the universe.

THE CAPABILITY OF ULTIMATE CAUSE

UC is capable of causing the universe to be as it is.

UC is capable of causing people to be as we are.

UC is capable of everything we and the tools we make are.

UC is capable of being aware of every person's every thought and feeling.

UC is capable of thinking my thoughts with me and through me.

UC is capable of having every person's whole life in memory beyond the universe.

[After reading an early manuscript of this book, a friend said, "It is about: what us outside the universe."]

THE RESULT OF KNOWING ULTIMATE CAUSE

The result of knowing Ultimate Cause is that now I think of UC as my companion. I am never alone. I think of UC experiencing with me and through me my every thought and feeling. UC knows and remembers everything about me. UC knows more about me than I know about myself. Ultimate Cause has me in virtual reality outside the universe.

I think of UC experiencing with me and through me; as I think about the galaxies of stars described by astronomy; as I think about the wonders of energy, electricity, magnetism, subatomic particles, molecules as described by physics; as I think about DNA, cells, metabolism as described by biology; as I think about human civilizations and cultures past, present, future; as I think about processes: weather, osmosis, the natural laws, gravity, thermodynamics, electromagnetism, photosynthesis—.

The idea of Ultimate Cause is the starting point of my philosophy. Through cause and effect, I relate everything to UC. When I do this, everything makes sense. UC made it as it is. UC made it to experience it, to enjoy it as a drama.

Knowing UC brings personal tranquility and social harmony. UC likes and enjoys everyone. So I should enjoy everyone, no matter how detrimental their actions.

The purpose of our being is for UC to experience with each of us our unique lives. A person may think he or she is not very important. But UC enjoys everyone. You are important to UC.

The government of the United States of America is based on the idea of Ultimate Cause that treats everyone alike. This is the basis of the equality of man. You may observe, as I have, that the sustaining citizens of stable societies function on the basis of Ultimate Cause.

INCIDENTS

Leaving a friend's home, I stopped and pointed to the wall and said, "We do not know how to make the atoms, molecules, energy, natural laws that make these materials possible. But there is that which does. Ultimate Cause knows all about them. UC caused all the processes that caused them. We can know Ultimate Cause as our companion."

Early in the morning just before Christmas 1980, I was driving on Highway 32 from Bonner Springs to teach in Kansas City, Missouri public schools. Beside me was a pickup truck outlined in lights. It was beautiful. I thought, "*The driver is proud of his truck. He is enjoying it. And I am enjoying it*". Then I thought, "*Ultimate Cause is enjoying it. UC is enjoying watching that man enjoying it. UC is enjoying the truck, that man and me. We are all enjoying the truck together. UC is enjoying it more than we are. UC sees the truck from other angles. UC knows all about that man deciding to put the lights on, how to put them on. UC knows the history of the lights, the people who made them and transported them.*"

SUMMARY

I think about Ultimate Cause of the whole universe, from subatomic particles to galaxies of stars, from DNA to cultures of mankind. Cause of the universe in our terms, thought about a universe, causing it to come into being, enjoys it, is our companion, and has complete memory of it. Ultimate Cause has our whole lives of thoughts, feelings, words, and deeds preserved in memory beyond the existence of the universe. When all is said and done memories remain. We infer cause of the universe from our knowledge of the universe. As our knowledge of the universe grows, so does our knowledge of its cause.

Everyone wonders what is back of and beyond the universe. Everyone wonders why the world? Why suffering and death? Where is the value? What is permanent?

We know the answers as we know cause of the universe. Religions, philosophies, and the sciences contribute to the idea of UC and are united in knowing Ultimate Cause.

If mankind is to be one people, it will be by orienting all thought to Ultimate Cause. If there is to be peace on earth and goodwill among men, it will be through thinking from the point of view of Ultimate Cause. UC likes and enjoys everyone. We should too. In our companionship with UC, we are companions of all people. As we like and enjoy everyone, we work to make stable social structures.

LOOK AROUND YOU

The earth is a big ball suspended in space. It operates by natural laws. It is made up of oceans, mountains, rivers, trees, grass, insects, animals, subatomic particles, molecules, cells, organisms, DNA, people, cultures. You and I do not know all about it. You and I did not make it. There is that which does know all about it and caused it to come into being. That is cause of the universe.

The sun is a huge atomic reactor ball of fire. It is one among billions of stars that make our Milky Way galaxy, which is one among billions of galaxies. You and I do not know all about them. You and I did not make them. But there is that which does know all about them and caused them. That is Ultimate Cause.

Around us are billions of people with many cultures, many thoughts, many languages, unique experiences. You and I do not know all about them. You and I did not cause them. But there is that which does know all about them and caused the processes in which they develop. That is Ultimate Cause.

Look at the back of your hand. Move your fingers and wrist. See the movement of the tendons and muscles. Feel on the inside above your wrist as you move your hand. Notice the movement of the tendons and muscles. Think about the intricate network of muscles that make the movement possible. Think about the nerve system, the blood system, bone structure, your brain and all your thoughts. All of this developed from a single cell, the fusion of two cells. All the instructions for your whole life were in that single cell. The trail of causes goes back to cause of causes, Ultimate Cause.

Look at the people around the world. You and I do not know all their thoughts and feelings, but there is that which does. That is Ultimate Cause.

HUMAN THOUGHT

We think about cause of the universe in human terms. We have no other way. But "cause of the universe" is not human, not a being, not part of the universe. We infer properties of Ultimate Cause from our knowledge of the universe. People have done this from the beginning of human thought. Around these inferences, religions, philosophies, sciences, and cultures develop. As our knowledge of the universe grows, so our view of what is beyond the universe changes, and our philosophies, religions, sciences, and cultures change.

DEVELOPMENT OF THIS BOOK

This book is in the form it is because I think it is the best way to present the idea of Ultimate Cause so it will blossom in the mind of the reader. I want the idea of UC to be more than just another thought passing through one's mind.

I have tried many approaches: chapters, story, scientific, religious, philosophical, analytical, as God, Creator—. I have written parts of it many times. I started writing this book in 1933.

In my notes, I wrote in 1934, "I will have to write this book this year or it will be a long time before I can do it, for I will be very busy from now on."

I spent the summer of 1940 in Washington, DC researching for the book in the Library of Congress. At that time I wrote to an observatory to find out: if by mapping the galaxies they could find where the universe started. They wrote back that they couldn't. They still can't.

This book is the product of a lifetime. Thoughts about Ultimate Cause will never end.

You may forget about cause of the universe. You may ignore Ultimate Cause. They are not going away.

II

KNOW ULTIMATE CAUSE

B
ANSWERING QUESTIONS

Another knock at the door, and B came in. I had known B for a long time, since she was a small girl. She is like a fresh breeze. She is perceptive, aware, and proficient. She intuitively knew from our comfortable attitudes what we had been talking about. She looked at me quizzically. I said, "Yes, we have been talking about C."

B 1
ULTIMATE CAUSE IN LITERATURE

She said, "You know, some people have said to you, 'Those are just your ideas.' They think no one else has had them. You might mention some of the places in literature where people have written about Ultimate Cause."

I said, "Certainly I want to do that."

Many people through the years have had ideas that fit Ultimate Cause. In the aggregate, their writings have included almost every aspect of Ultimate Cause. We can conceptualize Ultimate Cause from them when we include: automatic functions, natural laws, compression, long-term memory, processes ---.

A timeline is useful. It can show the development of idea. It shows how thinking has changed. Each generation is different. Each generation builds on the thoughts of the past. And yet some ideas go back a long way.

See Appendix 8 for thoughts of philosophers.

A. DRAMA   SHAKESPEARE

Shakespeare tells us we can look at our lives as a drama. He does not say for whom we play. Of course, we play for Ultimate Cause.

All the world's a stage,
And all the men and women merely players:
They have their exits and their entrances;
And one man in his time plays many parts.
Shakespeare — As you Like it Act II Scene 7 Line 139
(CIRCA 1600 AD)

These few lines tell us what our lives are about. We are in a drama. We are playing for Ultimate Cause. Ultimate Cause knows and enjoys every player, every act, every scene. We play, work, suffer and enjoy for C. We also play, work, enjoy and suffer for and with each other.

Drama has heroes and villains. In the interplay of life, each of us is saint and sinner, hero and villain. Our actions are beneficial to some and detrimental to others.

Each of us is free to make up our part within the milieu of our physical, mental, and cultural circumstances. C enjoys everything. We too may enjoy everything as we participate in the drama. We accept as part of the drama our own and others' joys, victories, sins, miseries, misfortunes. We enjoy the pleasures, comforts, and creature interplay with each other. We are privileged to know C. C is our companion. We have some of C's point of view.

B. THOMAS JEFFERSON GIVES THE IDEA OF ULTIMATE CAUSE, CREATOR, EQUALITY OF MAN.

DECLARATION OF INDEPENDENCE

"We hold these truths to be self-evident, that all men are created equal,
that they are endowed by their Creator with certain unalienable Rights;
that among these are Life, Liberty and the pursuit of Happiness."

– Thomas Jefferson, July 4, 1776

The Declaration says three things are obvious. One, there is a Creator of mankind. Second, all men are equal. To the Creator, we are equal. We should see others as equal to us. Third, all men have rights that are built into the universe, such as Life, Liberty, and the pursuit of Happiness.

We have our good life because we hold beyond dispute: that our Creator is, all men are equal and have rights that cannot be taken away: Life, Liberty, pursuit of Happiness --. Our government supports this view. It is important that we encourage all people around the world to have it. We may lose it if it does not prevail among all the people of the earth.

Thomas Jefferson in his letter to John Adams April 11, 1823 wrote about "ultimate cause":

"I hold (without appeal to revelation) that when we take a view of the universe in its parts, general or particular, it is impossible for the human mind not to perceive and feel a conviction of design, consummate skill, and infinite power in every atom of its composition. The movements of the heavenly bodies, so exactly held in their course by the balance of centrifugal and centripetal forces; the structure of our earth itself, with its distribution of lands, waters and atmosphere; animal and vegetable bodies, examined in all their minutest particles; insects, mere atoms of life, yet as perfectly organized as man or mammoth; the mineral substances, their generation and uses; it is impossible, I say, for the human mind not to believe, that there is in all this, design, cause, and effect, up to an ultimate cause, a fabricator of all things from matter and motion, their preserver, and regulator while permitted to exist in their present forms, and their regeneration into new and other forms."

The idea of Ultimate Cause is the foundation of our system of government. From it comes the equality of man before the government and in the eyes of the community.

C. IN THE BEGINNING

The ancient Hebrews had ideas that fit Ultimate Cause:

"In the beginning Elohim created the heavens and the earth.—
and Elohim said let there be—and Elohim saw that it was good."
(Genesis 1:1-3)

The idea of Elohim fits UC in many ways. Both were before "the heavens and the earth." Both in our terms thought of, wanted, designed, made, and found good what had been created (caused).

This passage has been known by multitudes for thousands of years. It comes from the crossroads of three continents. It is part of the cultures of Europe, Asia, and Africa. It is in the scriptures and folklore of three prominent religions: Judaism, Christianity, and Islam.

Moses, by tradition, wrote the Pentateuch, of which Genesis is a part. So Moses had this thought that fits UC. Other people before and since Moses have had thoughts that approach knowing UC. We do not attribute knowledge to people before it was discovered. People knew only the heavens and earth with their senses before tools such as telescopes and microscopes. The red shift on the spectrum of light from galaxies of stars that indicates the universe is expanding was not known till the 1900s.

D. PRESENCE AND AWARENESS

Another ancient writing is Psalm 139. It has the idea of the presence and awareness of Jehovah. It is compatible with our thoughts about UC. One can substitute UC for Jehovah. Here is a part of it:

"O Jehovah, You have searched me and known [me]. You know
my sitting down and my rising up. You understand my thoughts
from afar off. You know my path and my lying down, and are
acquainted [with] all my ways. For not a word on my tongue, but,
lo, O Jehovah, You know it all. –
---- "(Such) knowledge (is) too wonderful for me; it is high; I am
not able to reach it. Where shall I go from Your Spirit? --- If I go

*up to heaven, You (are) there; if I make my bed (in) hell behold
you are there! (If) I take the wings of the morning, dwelling in the
farthest part of the sea even there Your hand shall lead me, and
Your right hand shall seize me.*

*If I say: Surely the darkness shall cover me; even the night (shall
be) light around me.*

*Even the darkness will not be dark for You; but the night shines
as the day; the darkness (is) as the light. ----My bones were not
hidden from You when I was made in secret; ---Your eyes saw my
embryo; and in Your book all (my members) were written; -- And
how precious are Your thoughts to me, O Al (God)! How great is
the sum of them! (If) I should count them, they are more than the
sand; when I awake I am still with You."*

(From: "The Interlinear Bible, Hebrew, Greek, English", with
modification.)

This psalm has been known by multitudes of people for thousands
of years. It fits UC. Just substitute UC for Jehovah. UC shares our
experiences, thoughts, feelings, words and deeds. It contains the idea of
presence, being aware of everything and memory. It includes objectivity.
It hints that the world is a stage.

Thinking about the presence of Jehovah was important to the
psalmist. Thinking about UC is important for us.

{Bible quotations are mostly from the King James translations with
modifications from various translation, including "The Interlinear
Bible, Hebrew, Greek, English". }

E. COMMUNICATING

<u>Job</u>

"Then the Lord answered Job." (Job 38:1)

The story of Job contains the idea of a person communicating
with the Lord and the Lord responding. We communicate to C by
our thoughts. C communicates to us in our minds. We think UC's
response from our knowledge of the universe.

<u>We are our thoughts.</u>

"As a man thinks so is he." (Proverbs 23:7)

This also is an ancient observation that has been known by multitudes. It indicates we are our thoughts, our ideas, the virtual reality of our minds. Ultimate Cause to us is something like complete thought, complete virtual reality, Ultimate Reality itself. The universe is mortal, so ultimate reality is not part of the universe, yet envelops the universe.

The soul has been defined as the mind, as thought, as virtual reality. Our souls, our virtual reality, are in UC's virtual reality, in Ultimate Reality itself. We like life here on earth. UC caused it. UC provides whatever more there is. We have confidence in UC that it is all right.

F. BEFORE THE BEGINNING & TESTS OF TRUTH

My brother Willis thought about what UC did before the creation of the universe. He came up with this:

> "Genesis 0:0 Before the beginning,
> God created truth.
> Genesis 0:1 Then, all that followed,
> followed in truth."

What is this truth? Truth is the set of all of God's laws that governed the creation and existence of heaven and earth. The truth is the natural laws, rules by which the universe operates, which we are trying to approximate with what we call the laws of nature: thermodynamics, quantum physics, Einstein's Theory of Relativity. These are the unbreakable laws which include gravity, electromagnetism.

Then there are rules, commandments that are breakable, about which we have choices. We break the moral laws at our peril. I hope we develop our knowledge of both the unbreakable laws of nature and the moral laws so we live together with more peace and harmony.

TESTS OF TRUTH

There are four tests of truth from Jesus' statements, John 8:32, John 16:13, and John 16:2.

"You shall know the truth and the truth shall make you free."

"When he, the spirit of truth, is come, he will guide you into all truth…"

"They will put you out of the synagogue: yea, the time cometh, that whosoever kills you will think he does God service." (John 16:2)

The first test of truth is knowledge. Have we attained knowledge in the ensuing 2,000 years? Yes.

The second test of truth is freedom. Have we attained more freedom in the last 2,000 years? Yes.

The third test of truth is the fastest growing knowledge. It shows what truth is. What is the fastest growing knowledge? It is the sciences.

The fourth test of truth is being put out of the church for truth. It has come to pass. People have been put out of the church and killed for their knowledge of science. The sciences are the truth into which the comforter is leading us.

G. JESUS
QUOTATIONS OF JESUS THAT FIT ULTIMATE CAUSE:

Some of Jesus' description of the heavenly Father fit Ultimate Cause. Here are some of Jesus' sayings that are applicable to Ultimate Cause.

a. UC is always with us experiencing with us our every thought and feeling.
Jesus says heavenly Father is always with me, "I am not alone." 1.

b. UC does not judge, likes and enjoys everyone.
   Jesus says the "heavenly Father judges no one". 2.

c. UC knows everything about the universe and us.
   Jesus says the heavenly Father knows things no one else does. 3.

d. UC has our whole lives in memory beyond the universe.
   Jesus said His Father's estate has places to live. 4.

e. UC can change anything, everything.
   Jesus says nothing is impossible for God. 5.

f. When you know UC, you know you are in UC's memory beyond the universe.
   Jesus says eternal life is to know the heavenly Father. 6.

g. UC has built into the universe processes for development of complexity, intelligence and morality.
   Jesus taught morality and that heavenly Father is interested in morality. 7.

h. UC experiences with us our every thought, feeling, word, and deed.
   Jesus taught that whatever we do to others, we do to Him. 8.

i. UC likes and enjoys everyone as part of the drama.
   Jesus taught to love enemies, treat everyone equally as heavenly Father does. 9.

1. John 16:32 "I am not alone for the Father is with me"

2. John 5:22 --"the Father judges no one"--
   John 8:15 Jesus said, -- "I do not judge anyone."

3. Mark 13:31-32 "The heavens and the earth pass away. But concerning that day and the hour, no one knows, not the angels, those in Heaven, nor the Son, except the Father." Matthew 6:8 "—your Father knows what things you have need of, before you ask him." Matt. 10:29-32

"-— sparrows – one of them shall not fall to the ground without your Father." "But even the hairs of your head are all numbered." Luke 12: 6-7 "–sparrows – not one of them has been forgotten before God. But even the hairs of your head have all been numbered."

4. John 14:2 "In My Father's house are many places to live."

5. Matthew 19:26 "--with God all things are possible."

6. John 17: 1-3 Jesus in prayer said, "Father—this is the everlasting life, that they should know You. —"

The gospel is the good news that knowing heavenly Father is eternal life.

7. Matthew 23:11 "But the greater of you shall be your servant." John 16:13. "—when the Spirit of truth comes, He will guide you into all truth;--" Luke 4:17- 19 "He found the place where it was written, '(The) spirit of the Lord is upon me: therefor He anointed me to preach the gospel to (the) poor:--.'" John 8:32, "And you shall know the truth, and the truth shall set you free."

8. Matthew 25:40 "As long as you did (it) to one of these, the least of my brethren, you did (it) to Me."

9. Matthew 5:44-48 Jesus said "—I say to you, love your enemies, bless those cursing you, do well to those hating you, — that you may be sons of your Father who (is) in heaven: for he causes His sun to rise on evil and on good, and sends rain on (the) just and (the) unjust. – Be ye therefore be perfect, even as your Father in heaven is perfect."

MORE TO COME

Jesus said to his followers, "I have yet many things to say unto you, but ye cannot bear them now. Howbeit when he, the Spirit of truth, is come, he will guide you into all truth" (John 16:12-13). "You shall know the truth and the truth will make you free" (John 8:32).

Jesus indicates his work is part of processes. The processes are the developing of mankind's understanding, and developing of social structures so everyone has the best possible life. One of the processes is our increasing knowledge of our environment. We know more all the time. Our models of the universe, the Virtual Realities in our minds, are becoming more and more accurate. We are freer, in that we can do more. More people are living longer and better than ever before. UC made processes part of the universe.

We have much to learn, much to do. The earth's resources are being depleted and polluted. There are conflicts among people all over the earth. People are starving. People are maiming and killing others. People are divided over religion. There is disagreement about God. Hindus, Buddhists, Muslims, Jews, and Christians are being attacked.

Still needed is development of the idea and feeling that all the people of the world are one people. Jesus taught this in his story of the Good Samaritan, (Luke 10:30) and in Matthew 5:43-48 "love your enemies—be perfect as the Father in heaven is perfect."

To think of ourselves as one people, we need a common understanding of the universe. We need a common view of what is back of the universe. And we need a common view of why we exist, the reason for our being. A common understanding of the universe involves universal education. Television and the Internet are helping. People all over the world have the opportunity to know the universe from subatomic particles to galaxies of stars, from DNA to the many cultures of mankind. People are seeing the universe is processes, recycling, mortal. People are seeing that mortality is the reason for morality. People are seeing that the earth is a stage. We are the players developing moral cultures.

A common understanding of what is back of the universe comes from thinking in terms of cause and effect. Most people accept that there is cause for every phenomenon. So they accept that there is cause of the universe. People are united when they think in terms of Ultimate Cause. People are united in inferring that Ultimate Cause in causing the universe would have something like our experience making things. We make things because we need them, or to experience and enjoy them. We know of no reason Ultimate Cause would need the universe or us. That leaves the reason for Ultimate Cause causing the universe and us is to enjoy and experience with each of us our unique life.

People are united through Ultimate Cause when they think of Ultimate Cause experiencing with everyone his or her thoughts, feelings, words, and deeds. In our common relationship to UC, we are related to each other.

When we make things that function on their own (automatically), we don't need to intervene, but we can. So cause of the universe can but does not need to intervene. The processes of the universe suit the purpose of their cause.

Jesus in prayer said, "Father—this is the life eternal that they might know thee --." (John 17:1-3).

The Gospel is the good news that knowing heavenly Father is life eternal. The good news is that you can know Ultimate Cause. UC has the total memory of each of our lives preserved outside the universe. When we know Ultimate Cause, we have personal tranquility and participate in social harmony.

Worship, (prayer, study, meditation) is thinking about and coordinating our ideas with the greatest we know. Worship is coordinating our thoughts and actions to Ultimate Cause. It is developing our relationship with (our thoughts of) our companion UC.

We want to worship as Jesus did. Jesus worshipped the heavenly Father that to us is cause of the universe.

See APPENDIX 6 for more on Jesus.

H. PETER
ALL PEOPLE ARE EQUAL.

Peter said, "—God has shown me that I should not call any man common or unclean" (Acts10:28). See story Acts 10:9–15.

This coordinates with thoughts of Ultimate Cause. UC likes everything about the world and all people. We are to enjoy (enjoyment is love) every other person. To enjoy others, it helps to see life as a drama.

We need this lesson today. Many people separate themselves from others. Many look down on others.

I. PAUL

1) Paul wrote about Jesus being "the first born among many brethren" (Romans 8:29).

   We are brethren with each other and brethren of Jesus when we share thoughts.

2) Paul wrote "Be not overcome of evil, but overcome evil with good" (Romans 12:21).

   We need to win our fellow man to good by example. Ultimate Cause has built development of morality by moral science into the universe.

3) "—you are saved through faith" (Ephesians 2:8).

   When one's thoughts and feelings are coordinated to satisfaction in knowing UC: that is faith and being saved. Without logic, one's faith is vulnerable, as Mother Teresa's story indicates. Faith is thought. It is feeling. One is saved when one in thought and feeling knows Ultimate Cause. Those who are aware of Ultimate Cause are satisfied with their lives and death. To them, everything makes sense. One is saved from despair to personal tranquility and social harmony by being aware of Ultimate Cause.

4). Paul on Mars Hill.

"—Paul stood on Mars Hill and said — I found an altar with this inscription, TO THE UNKNOWN GOD. Whom therefore you ignorantly worship, him declare I unto you. God that made the world

and all things therein, seeing that he is Lord of heaven and earth, dwells not in temples made with hands; neither is worshipped with men's hands, as though he needed any thing, seeing he gives to all life, and breath, and all things; And hath made of one blood all nations of men that dwell on all the face of the earth, —he is not far from every one of us: for in him we live, and move, and have our being"— (Acts 17:22-28)

Paul gives a good description of UC. UC caused the universe and all things therein, does not live in temples made with hands, is not worshipped with men's hands, does not need anything. UC is not far from any one of us. UC is experiencing with us our every thought and feeling and has us in memory beyond the existence of the universe; made of one blood all nations of men.

Paul did not mention processes and natural laws. Long in the future was (the development of science) knowledge of compression of information in DNA (in eggs, stem cells, ---); computers and widespread automatic operations. People thought of some mysterious, God doing things directly rather than as chains of causes and effects to Ultimate Cause.

J. REVELATION

The book of Revelation is a drama. Violence makes the drama. It indicates a violent end. Apparently, our sun will explode as other stars have. Ultimate Cause remains. .

K. RELIGIONS OF MANKIND

Ultimate Cause of the universe likes and enjoys all that people think and do. UC views all people do as drama. So UC likes and enjoys all the religious activities of mankind.

Religions use revelations, dreams, visions, rituals, traditions and art.

Some consider knowledge of nature the foundation of religious belief. This fits in with the idea of Ultimate Cause that we know by inference from our knowledge of the universe.

Most everyone has thoughts about cause of the universe (as they know the universe). The more we know about the universe with our constantly increasing scientific knowledge the better we can think about Ultimate Cause. Religions can help people think in terms of UC.

When people's thinking is UC-centric, they develop democratic government, morality and ethics based on natural laws. The work is to develop UC-centric thinking so all the people of the world can develop democratic culture. Religions will decide their place in this work.

Religions have traditionally played major rolls in education, government, morality and ethics. They may play a major roll in orienting all thought to UC and in developing natural moral laws.

L. POETRY

For what are men better than sheep or goats
That nourish a blind life within the brain,
If knowing God, they lift not hands of prayer
Both for themselves and those who call them
Friend?
Tennyson: Morte d'Arthur L. 247.

We are to rise above the animal life to know UC and share out knowledge of UC with others.

M. PHILOSOPHERS

Each of us has our own philosophy. What others write and say are resources.

1. Objectivity is shown by Epictetus. He said to his master that if he kept twisting his leg, it would break.

2. The Deists had the idea that the Creator is separate from the universe, designed and started the development of the universe, and left it running as a watchmaker does a watch. This is the idea that the universe operates by processes according to natural laws. They thought about natural moral laws that should be found and used as the basis for morality, ethics, and justice. The government should base laws and justice on natural laws. These ideas fit Ultimate Cause. They are the foundation of the government of the United States of America.

3. Erasmus Darwin, Charles Darwin's grandfather, wrote in 1794 about the possibility of the world having developed from very small beginnings. He thought of the Cause of Causes, which is another symbol for cause of the universe. Here is his writing:

> "The world itself might have been generated, rather than created; that is, it might have been gradually produced from very small beginnings, increasing by the activity of its inherent principles, rather than by a sudden evolution by the whole by the Almighty fiat. What a magnificent idea of the infinite power of the great architect! The Cause of Causes! Parent of Parents! Ens Entium! For if we can compare infinities, it would seem to require a greater infinity of power to cause the cause of effects, than to cause the effects themselves."
>
> Internet: Erasmus Darwin cause of causes. Zoonomia

What a description of Ultimate Cause. And written 200 years ago!

4. David Hume in *An Inquiry Concerning Human Understanding,* dated 1748, wrote that the idea of a cause of the universe is worthy of some consideration. Although he doubted that a cause can be known only by an effect. He points out that a cause can be known only as far as the effect warrants. There has to be a one to one relationship between the cause and the effect.

We are not to attribute to cause more than is known from the effect. (The cause is also adequate to cause the effect.)

We are not from a completely inferred cause make inference about the effect (from which we inferred the cause).

[Read about David Hume in *Modern Philosophy* p. 445-550]

N. PROCESSES

"The general theory of evolution... assumes that in nature there is great, unital, continuous and everlasting process of development, and that all natural phenomena without exception...are subject to the same great law of causation."
Ernest Haeckel, Frei Wissenschaft und frei Lehre, 1878

Haeckel's writing about "some great law of causation," points to Ultimate Cause. UC is cause of natural laws.

O. PERSPECTIVE INSCRIPTION ON A TOMB

"As you are now so once was I
Someday you will be as I."

I have been in all the stages of life up to the point I am now as you read this. I have been a newborn, a child, a youth, student, laborer, parent, grandparent, great-grandparent, sick, well, robust, weak. You may think of this on my tomb, one day. We are part of the processes of the universe.

I have had a complete life; in knowing the universe as the scientific method shows it, in experiencing the culture of my time and place, in observing other cultures, in knowing the great thoughts of thinking people of the past and present.

Nothing has been denied me. I have great friends, a great family, parents, grandparents, relatives, wife, children, grandchildren, their spouses and children. I have all the resources anyone could desire.

I grew up and worked on a frugal, productive, horse-powered farm. My mother was a master homemaker of Kansas, my father a Reno County commissioner. I started in a one-room country school, attended a large high school with physics, chemistry, and mathematics. I studied philosophy, social sciences, and statistics in college. In seminary, I learned about religion and became a Presbyterian minister. I served as pastor of four churches over a period of forty years. I taught in the Kansas City, Missouri public schools for fifteen years. I have walked behind cultivators pulled by horses, worked in factories, traveled around the world, written computer programs (in APL).

P. FREE

Philosophers can by the sequence of cause and effect orient all thought with Ultimate Cause, so everything is logical and makes sense. Philosophy has been defined as the search for Ultimate Cause.

Scientists can by the sequences of cause and effect orient everything to Ultimate Cause, so everything makes sense.

Religions can orient everything to Ultimate Cause so everything makes sense. Religions can be united in Ultimate Cause. When they are, people can work together to promote abundant living for everyone. They can be one community in their common companionship with Ultimate Cause.

When our everyday experiences are oriented to Ultimate Cause, everything makes sense.

Thus, philosophy, science, religion, and ordinary life experiences are united in one perspective when we know Ultimate Cause.

Those who think in terms of Ultimate Cause support the free use of the scientific method to explore everything in the universe. They support the free use of reason, unhindered by taboos, fear of mysteries, imaginations, superstitions. They support free participation in religions, because they are meaningful to people, as long as they do not interfere with the freedom of others.

Ultimate Cause knows and enjoys all people's thoughts and feelings about God, the gods, religious practices. We can enjoy them too. UC enjoys everyone and everything people do. We, too, may enjoy everyone and the things they do. It is all a drama. The more we know about the universe, the better we know Ultimate Cause.

B said, "That is enough to show some of the history of the idea of Ultimate Cause. Many people have thought of Ultimate Cause. They did not go on to develop the idea so people would have the perspective of Ultimate Cause. You are here developing the idea of UC so people can think in terms of UC and communicate with each other about UC."

The Appendix has more about the development of the ideas of Ultimate Cause.

B 2
EVIL

After reflecting, B said, "I think you might say something about the idea of Evil."

I said, "B, I love you for your seeming innocence. You are a subtle scalawag. You know very well what thinking in terms of Ultimate Cause does to the idea of evil."

I continued, "Simply put, nothing about the universe is evil to UC. Nothing about the universe hurts UC. UC is not part of the universe. The universe is just like UC wants it. The universe is processes of constant change. It is mortal. Structures of subatomic particles, molecules, cells and structures of life, human cultures -- are constantly being made, are disintegrating, and new structures being formed. Everything that happens in the universe is part of processes and drama for UC to experience and enjoy. Nothing in the universe is evil to UC.

"On the other hand, people work to live as long and well as possible. Anything that interferes with this work is considered evil. The processes that lead to mortality, the processes of recycling, and anything that causes pain is evil. People are called evil who intentionally interfere with other people's effort to defer mortality.

"We who think in terms of UC do the best we can and accept mortality. We realize UC is experiencing it with us, and remembers it all beyond the existence of the universe. We realize we are part of a continual development of knowledge and thinking skills.

"As those who went before us left to make place for us, so we leave to make room for the next generation. They will know more and think better.

"Our work of developing morality and ethics is a drama. We work to get all people to live together tranquilly, harmoniously, and dynamically. We work to encourage everyone to think about Ultimate Cause and have the point of view, the perspective, of cause of the universe.

"To UC and those who have UC's point of view the universe is dynamic, change, recycling, and drama. Those who have UC's point of view put their effort into making religions, sciences, philosophies, and infrastructures so everyone on earth has the best possible life.

"When people think of God as part of the universe, then God is like man, there is evil to God. God is good. God does not want death and recycling. There is a devil working against God. God is fighting evil. Then God enlists people in fighting evil. In this view the natural laws are evil, not what God wants: 'the wolf will lie down with the lamb.' (Isaiah 11:6). God punishes those who do not believe in him, by disasters such as earthquakes, tornadoes, droughts, epidemics -- which have been termed 'acts of god'.

"When we think of God as UC, (as cause of the universe as it is, as cause of the natural laws); then there is no evil to God. Then Ockham's Razor applies and we do not employ a plurality of concepts beyond necessity. We do not make things more complicated than necessary. Mortality and recycling account for our difficulties. We accept mortality as UC made it and enjoy the experiences it brings. We work to make the best possible life for everyone on earth by morality and infrastructures that are realistic to human nature and our earth environment.

"Though UC is not mortal and not morale, UC has complete empathy with each person. UC experiences with each person every thought and feeling. So UC experiences all the pain, suffering and misery with each person."

B 3
UC AND GOD

"After some silence, B said, "You know you haven't explained the idea of UC compared to the idea of God."

I said, "You bring up an important point. UC is of a different order than God.

UC is a concept of rational cause-and-effect inductive thinking, inferring UC from knowledge of the universe. It is up to each person to study and understand for him- or herself.

God is often a concept of faith, hope, love, revelation, accepting authority, submission."

Only you know what you think and believe about God. You think members of your group have the same ideas you do. But one is never certain what other people are thinking.

We do have records of what some people have written about what they thought and believed. We have records of what some people have done in the name of God

GOD

Encyclopedia Britannica 1959 has this to say about God:

"GOD, the common Teutonic word for a personal object of religious worship. It is thus, like Gr. Theos, and Lat. Deus, applied to all superhuman beings of heathen mythologies who exercise power over nature and man; and also to images of supernatural beings or trees, pillars, etc. used as symbols. The word, 'god' on the conversion of the Teutonic races to Christianity, was applied to the one Supreme Being and to the person of the Trinity."

"According to the *Oxford English Dictionary*, concerning god, the original may be found in two Aryan roots, both of the form *gheu,* one of which means "to invoke," and the other "to pour"; the last is used of sacrificial offerings. The word would thus mean the object either of religious invocation or of religious worship by sacrifice".

****

God is anything anyone wants to call God. Think of all the ideas of God people have had: the Greek gods, Egyptian gods, the gods of the people of Central and South America, of Africa, Hindu, Buddha, animist. God can be a statue, a person, ruler, creator, a hero, savior. Ideas of God are developed from dreams, revelations, authoritative writings, fears, hopes, desire for being saved from difficulties, wanting to know what caused the universe.

Mankind's ideas about God are attempts to understand what his life is about. Religions and cultures are developed around ideas about God. Notice the differences in the cultures where the predominant idea is Hindu, Buddhist, Jewish, Christian, Islamic, Deist. Cultures are often a mixture of ideas about God.

The United States of America is called Christian. The idea of the providence and guidance of God as revealed in Jesus Christ is strong. Yet the idea that God (UC) made the universe to operate by natural laws has prevailed. People are responsible for learning the natural laws and observing them.

In the three theistic religions (Hebrew, Christian, Islam) God gives commands, rewards those who obey, punishes those who disobey. God is mollified by repentance, sacrifice, prayer, belief.

God is providential. God has opposition. God chooses people to be his people. God wants his people to oppose evil. (Everywhere, there are people who accept the religion of their culture but actually function on the basis of the world as it is, caused by Ultimate Cause).

Religions that developed around the ideas of God have been of service to mankind. They provide community, faith, hope, love, and inspiration. They educate, heal, give meaning to life, provide moral base, and promote infrastructures that make life better for many people.

Each of us develops the philosophy, science, and religion of the culture in which each of us lives, generally where we were born.

What people accept as knowledge of nature is the foundation of their philosophy, religion, culture, civilization. Our knowledge of nature makes possible and limits our cultures, religions, sciences, and philosophies. Our language enables and limits our culture, religions, sciences, and philosophies.

As much good as religions and the ideas about God do, there are problems. There is no objective view of God. Different groups of people have different revelations, moralities and authorities.

Views of God have been and are divisive. People have used the idea of God, even claim God is guided them to wage war, kill, enslave, limit research and education. Some claim they are fighting evil in the name of God. Some people believe God will reward them if they die killing opponents.

These ideas come from the idea that God is good, is holy, is moral, gives commands, judges, rewards, punishes, and is providential. God's people should be like God. God's purpose is to have people think of him and obey his commands. God has opposition, is in conflict with evil. People claim God is guiding them to fight evil.

People are as their God. I do not think Ultimate Cause as God. Ultimate Cause known by inference from our knowledge of the universe as capability to cause the universe to be as it is; is like nature, the knowledge of which is the foundation of religion. Religions deal with mortality and morality (how to live as long and swell as we can). We need to know nature and nature's cause (Ultimate Cause) as the foundation, as the base for God of faith, hope, and love (charity).

My concern is that mankind does not have a unifying philosophy, a unifying religion, a common acceptance of science; nor is there a unifying view of science, religion, and philosophy. The people of the world are divided into competing groups with various views of God, morality, religion, science, and philosophy. The result is that there are people unnecessarily miserable, dying due to famine, disease, inadequate infrastructures, conflict, and prejudice.

The solution is in knowing "cause of the universe," Ultimate Cause. The solution is for everyone to have personal tranquility and promote social harmony in knowing that Ultimate Cause is their companion. It is in unification of all people in common companionship with UC. (Actually, this is already happening in many areas where the underlying ideas of UC are observed, subconsciously if not consciously).

ULTIMATE CAUSE

Ultimate Cause is capability to cause the universe to be as it is. We know UC by inference from our knowledge of the universe according to the rules of cause and effect.

When we know cause of the universe, we know what life is about. UC likes and enjoys everyone, is not to be invoked or worshipped by sacrifice. UC is everyone's companion, aware of every thought and feeling. The purpose of our being is so UC can experience with each person his or her unique life. The universe and life of mankind is a drama UC enjoys.

Ideas of Ultimate Cause are limited to inferences from our knowledge of the universe. As our knowledge of the universe increases, we conceptualize UC better. People are able to conceptualize UC when they know the universe with tools, analyze their own experience making things, learn to infer cause from effect, then infer cause of the universe from their knowledge of the universe. We are careful to infer to UC only what our knowledge of the universe warrants. We limit our ideas of UC to a one-to-one relationship between effect and cause.

The ordinary idea of God does not fit UC. UC is not a being, not holy, not good (in terms of human life), is not to be propitiated by sacrifice, is not a spirit, not moral, not fighting evil.

We may think of worshipping UC if we think of worship as studying the universe, inferring UC from our knowledge of the universe, thinking of our companionship with UC, thinking and laughing to UC, thinking UC's point of view and UC's response from our knowledge of the universe. In other words, worship is thinking about the universe and its relationship to UC.

The universe exists for UC to enjoy, not for our benefit. Although we can enjoy the universe, something like UC does when our thinking is UC-centric, and we have the point of view of UC.

Our job is to learn the natural laws and use them to develop rational living that provides the best possible life for everyone on earth. Our job is to work with others to make infrastructures that make life as good as possible for everyone.

The purpose of our being is so UC can enjoy the unique life of each person. The universe is processes. Man's life is a drama of developing from instinctive to rational living. UC likes and enjoys everyone and everything, including ideas about God and religious practices.

All over the world, since the beginning of rational thought, there have been people who have had the idea of cause and effect up to the idea of cause of all they knew. Some had a tradition of it. But I know of no record of their developing the idea of UC. The idea of cause and effect was blended into the idea of God. Hence, they missed knowing UC as their companion, sharing their every thought and feeling, and remembering their whole lives beyond the universe. They did not known UC well enough so they could laugh to UC, knowing UC was experiencing their whole lives with them and knew them better than they knew themselves.

Many people have the idea of UC in their subconscious minds. They use the stories of God as culture and moral ethical base. They see the church with its services as community, cultural, educational, faith, and hope.

REASONS PEOPLE HAVE NOT DEVELOPING THE IDEA OF ULTIMATE CAUSE

There are numerous reasons why the idea of Ultimate Cause has not been developed before.

One is that people claim they already know Ultimate Cause because that is just God and we know God. UC has nothing more for us.

Thomas Aquinas does this. He gives five proofs of first cause and says, "One is therefore forced to suppose some first cause, to which everyone gives the name 'God'." This closes thinking about UC. There is no reason to think about UC.

A second is that God is moral, good, holy, gives commands, judges, rewards, punishes (on earth and beyond), and chooses people to be his people. Moses is the supreme example of this. He came down from the mountain and said, "Thus saith the Lord God of Israel" (Exodus 32:27).

We still have people saying they have God's message. They speak for God. Their actions are guided by God. They see and proclaim that there is no reason to think about UC.

Of course, Ultimate Cause likes and enjoys everyone regardless of who they are and what they do. UC made the life of man to develop and be as it is with the processes of mortality, recycling and development of people's minds over generations.

The processes of mortality and recycling are what many call evil. They are however our problem. They make the drama. We spend our time and effort delaying mortality. But finally we accept mortality and recycling as part of the reliable processes, part if the design of the universe.

Third is that mankind is caught up in fighting evil with God. They think man is in rebellion against God. God is fighting evil: commanding, judging, punishing and rewarding. Man needs to repent and turn to God. Man needs to submit, obey God's laws and fight evil.

From the point of view of UC the universe and life of man are a drama of development.

There are many more reasons why the idea of UC has not been developed. People think: the heavens and earth just are, so there is no cause. God is constantly sustaining the universe. God needs the universe and man. God knows the future so the universe is not a drama. People fear the loss of morality if the idea of UC is accepted (not realizing that the idea of equality of man and democracy is based on Ultimate Cause). Some people have difficulty thinking of cause of the universe beyond the universe. It has been difficult for people to think of the earth and sky as not being.

People cease thinking about UC and say. "It is beyond my thinking." People are influenced by powerful, charismatic leaders, and traditions that oppose and/or ignore the idea of UC. People get caught up with enthusiasm in campaigns.

The vocabulary, knowledge, and thinking skill adequate for people to conceptualize Ultimate Cause have been developed only recently. People have tried to conceptualize cause of the universe for a long time.

The first chapters of Genesis indicate the attempt to know Ultimate Cause.

Thales (624-550 BC) thought about one Ultimate Reality, which he thought was water. (We now think the universe is made up of energy in different forms.) Now we can think beyond the universe about Ultimate Cause.

DIFFERENCES

Briefly consider the difference in the idea of God and of Ultimate Cause.

Ideas about God are so varied we can only point out what some people think about God. Some people think that God created, maintains, sustains, and intervenes in the life of man directly, immediately, continually. God is providential to those he chooses. He ignores, even brings harm to others. God has been reputed to have helped people drive others out of their land.

Some people think man is in rebellion against God. God has opposition, is fighting evil, and enlists man in conflict with evil. God communicates by prophets. God is known by revelation and through sacred writing.

Nahum 1:2 "God (is) jealous, and Jehovah revenges; Jehovah revenges and is a possessor of wrath. Jehovah takes vengeance against His foes, and He keeps (wrath) against His enemies."

Ultimate Cause is none of those.

Ultimate Cause caused the universe including the earth and man to develop automatically by the processes of natural laws. Man is in the process of learning the natural laws and to live by them rationally. Man is developing from instinctive to rational living.

When we (who think in terms of UC) have difficulties, instead of blaming the devil or of God punishing us; we look for inadequate social structures, people not helping make life good for everyone, or people causing difficulty. When things go well we notice there are good people and good social structures around.

UC caused the universe to experience and enjoy it as a drama. UC is every person's companion, experiencing with each person his/her complete life of thoughts and feelings, and preserves it all in memory beyond the existence of the universe. We only need to become aware of UC's companionship. In our common companionship with UC, we are companions with everyone on earth—all who have ever lived and will live.

People ask, what happens to religion when people think in terms of Ultimate Cause?

Religions teach about the universe and the inferences we make to know Ultimate Cause. There is no end to knowledge of the universe. There is no end to knowledge about mankind and cultures. There is no end to thinking about UC's enjoyment of people, all they are thinking and feeling. There is no end to our work to make life as good as possible for every person on earth by infrastructures and personal responsibilities.

There is no end to creating and maintaining community, love, ritual, art.

Religion can work to develop morality and laws that fit the way people are, that are according to natural laws. There is work to wisely organize and operate society; and use the resources of the earth so future generations may have the best possible life. Studying, thinking, working, and enjoying will take at least a day a week. Some time each day should be spent thinking about UC and our work to make living as good as possible for all people. So the whole of our lives and work is oriented around Ultimate Cause. All our activities, including our work, should be oriented toward the good of mankind.

Ultimate Cause of the universe, known by inference from our knowledge of the universe, should be the foundation of our thinking. Everyone should coordinate his or her ordinary daily thinking, science, philosophy, and religion with UC. UC is the coordinating center for all thought. All thought is logically related when it is coordinated with Ultimate Cause that causes the universe to be as it is with processes.

UC likes and enjoys everyone and everything about the universe and life of man. It is all drama for UC to experience and enjoy. UC does not judge. UC does not limit human exploration. UC is everyone's companion. We are companions with everyone on earth in our common companionship with UC.

Morality and ethics are our problem. It is the problem of providing the infrastructures to provide a good life for everyone on earth. Policies that lead to overpopulation, starvation, and degradation of environment are immoral. Punishments that do not protect society are immoral. UC preserves the memory of everyone's whole life of thoughts, feelings, words, and deeds beyond the existence of the mortal universe without judgment.

SEMANTICS

Semantic problems (the meaning of words and their changing meaning) are common. Both the speaker (writer) and the hearer (reader) need to have the same meaning for there to be accurate communication. Often, extensive explanations are needed.

We think with our words and their meaning. Our vocabulary is crucial to thinking. We have difficulty thinking in areas where we have no vocabulary. (There is evidence that, generally, we do not have ideas and do not think in areas where we do not have adequate language. In other words, we need language that has vocabulary and syntax structure to think in any area.) To think of UC, we need vocabulary adequate to think about Ultimate Cause.

There is the problem of equating words. Synonyms have different meaning. God does not mean Ultimate Cause exactly. So we need the words "Ultimate Cause" and we need commonly agreed upon definitions.

The vocabulary about UC enriches everyone's life. Repetition develops vocabulary. I hope there is enough repetition for you to think in terms of UC.

We seek meaning in life through experience. When all is said and done, memories remain. So it is with us and UC. Our whole lives are in UC's memory beyond the existence of the universe. It all depends on UC.

Much of the idea of God is quite anthropocentric. The idea of Ultimate Cause is completely UC-centric.

SEE APPENDIX 4 for more about GOD.

Z

At this point, Z spoke up. Z had come in about the time T had. He had heard the conversation. We call him Z. His name is Zeek. He was an old friend. I say old. He was not old. He was in the prime of life. He had been around the Horn. There was not much that Z had not done.

INTELLECTUAL REVOLUTION

Z said, "We are living in an intellectual revolution. It is changing life for most people around the world. Some people are actively participating. Some are resisting. Some are fighting it. The revolution is in tools and knowledge gained by tools. It involves tools for the mind: logic, mathematics, semantics, methodology, physics, chemistry, biology, psychology, sociology. It involves mechanical tools such as microscopes, telescopes, measuring devices, telephones, television, and computers ---.

"The revolution is in what people think. People without tools know only with their senses. They know heaven [sky] and earth. People using tools know there is more than heaven [sky] and earth. The universe is our solar system, galaxies of stars, electricity, magnetism, energy, subatomic particles, life, processes, mortality, natural laws, and human cultures ---.

"The thought revolution involves our view of what is back of the universe. We infer what is back of the universe from our view of the universe. So as our view of the universe changes, we change our view of what is back of the universe.

"Before tools, some people thought that heaven and earth were directly created by a being. That being communicated directly, through inspired writings, prophets, revelations, visions, dictation. That being providentially cared for people, and worked miracles for chosen people.

"With tools, people think of the universe developing. Cause of the universe is not part of the universe, is not a being. Cause of the universe is known by inference from our knowledge of the universe."

Z continued, "The idea of God; giving laws and commandments, judging, rewarding in heaven and assigning to hell is strong. To question it is such a taboo that in some situations, people fear for their social relations, livelihood, even their lives.

"Moses came down from the mountain and said he had direct messages from God. He gave God's commandments and laws. They were enforced by social controls, even death. The idea of God's laws is strong today among Jews, Christians, and Muslims.

"There is a semantic problem. When the word 'God' is used, one does not know what is meant. Does it mean God as thought of by people who think like people of Israel, Christianity, Islam, Hindu, ---? Does it mean God as those whose thinking is fundamental, moderate, liberal, evangelical, or radical?

"You are developing the idea of 'cause of the universe' we know with tools. Others have thought about it, but have not developed the idea. But it has been gradually developing. You think the time has come to directly think in terms of cause of the universe."

I said, "Yes. Jesus included the properties of UC in his thoughts about the Father in heaven. Thomas Jefferson and others have worked the ideas about UC into the framework of our country. We work on the basis of processes and natural laws. And as has been pointed out, the sustaining people of stable cultures function on the basis of Ultimate Cause. Take, for example, the equality of people to the government. It took a long time to eliminate slavery and to include women as voters. But it happened. It is recognized that legislatures should develop moral and ethical laws according to the will of the people, life as it is. There is the idea that the criminal justice system should aim at protecting society and habituating, not punishment. There is the idea of developing social structures that provide everyone the best possible life.

"The development of knowledge of the universe by tools has been a gradual process over hundreds of years. As an example, it is said that the Italian physician Marcello Malpighi, founder of microscopic anatomy, was the first to see red blood cells and capillaries. He was born March 10, 1628.

"It seems to me that the ideas of God will gradually develop into thinking in terms of Ultimate Cause. The idea of Ultimate Cause has been developing for generations. Every generation adjusts their idea of God to their knowledge of the universe.

"Ultimate Cause made people as we are. UC enjoys the ideas people have of God. UC enjoys all that people are thinking and doing in religions.

"People say they do not have time or energy to think about Ultimate Cause. For centuries, it has been thought appropriate to dedicate one day a week to think about philosophy, religion, art, beauty; to enjoy life with family and friends; to orient life; to participate in community. We should continue the practice and use part of one day a week to incorporate UC into our thinking.

"With logical certainty, you now know UC. UC is with you. UC is your companion. You know the reason for your being is for UC to experience with you and through you your unique life. Your whole life is preserved in UC's memory. Think to UC. Put your communication to UC into words. Think UC's response from your knowledge of the universe.

"Life is a drama. I often find myself doing things that are dramatic. Some of them others do not think are appropriate. I am sure UC enjoys the drama. Many times a day, I think to UC and I think of UC's response. We know UC's response from our knowledge of the universe.

"I laugh when I think of UC thinking my thoughts with me. How funny, seemingly absurd, and wonderful that cause of the whole universe of galaxies of stars thinks my thoughts with me. This is not ego. This is the capability of Ultimate Cause."

B 4
PROOF

After considerable time reflecting, B said, "You know, there is another thing you might take up. It is the idea of proof. I hear a lot about it. People keep saying 'Prove it... You can't prove the universe is rational... You can't prove there is always a cause for phenomena... You can't prove the universe is made up of processes... You can't prove Ultimate Cause'."

I said, "You are right. We want proof. We need proof. Let's consider three things about proof. What we mean by proof. The limitations of proof. The proofs of UC."

WHAT WE MEAN BY PROOF

Proof is a personal thing for each of us. Each of us decides what is proven to us. No one but you can say it is proven to you. No matter what anyone else says, you decide what is proven to you. Each of us is a closed mental system. We cannot get outside of our minds. We are limited to our experience, ideas, and thinking skills. We are constantly modifying our virtual reality with new experiences and ideas.

Cause and effect relationships are primary in human thought. A baby randomly waving hands and legs hits something, making it move. It may even rattle. It happens over and over again. The baby develops the idea that hitting something has an effect. Thus, each of us develops the axiom of cause and effect by induction from many observations.

When we are ill, we want to know the cause. We are constantly dealing with cause-and-effect relationships. From these experiences, we are convinced that phenomena have cause.

Logic and mathematics are games played with symbols. Information is substituted for the symbols. The game is then played with data. Practical problems are solved. An example: we play with letters a, b, c, d, x, y, z --. We play with equations $a + b = c$, $a/b = c$, $a * b = c$. We have rules of operation: addition, subtraction, ---. We substitute information into the equation: $a + b = c$, if $a = 2$, and $b = 5$, then $2 + 5 = c$, then $c = 7$.

Mathematics and logic guide us in making bridges, electricity, computers, Medicines, sending men to the moon and bringing them back. When we study logic and proofs in mathematics, we practice being convinced. We experience proving. We become aware of the process of being convinced. I remember in the ninth and tenth grades, standing at the blackboard, looking at proofs. It was effective. I remember the experiences distinctly. I learned to think in terms of proof.

LIMITS OF PROOF

Proof is a personal decision. Each person decides what is proven to him or herself. We may rely on authorities. We verify ideas with our associates. We may accept our emotions, the way we feel, as proof. Each of us is a closed, mental virtual reality system, which we develop from our experience. We cannot get outside of ourselves to verify it, but we communicate with others to verify that they have similar thoughts.

PROOF OF ULTIMATE CAUSE

One proof for Ultimate Cause is the one-to-one relationship of cause and effect. Our experience is that everything we deal with is caused. So the universe is caused. It has cause. We call cause of the universe Ultimate Cause.

The syllogism can be used to logically prove Ultimate Cause. By experience, we have the proposition: "For every phenomenon, there is cause. The universe is a phenomenon. Therefore, for the universe, there is cause.' We may associate any symbol to cause of the universe, but choose Ultimate Cause, UC or C.

DIAGRAM

This diagram shows the one-to-one relationship between our experiences making something to the experience Ultimate Cause would have had making the universe.

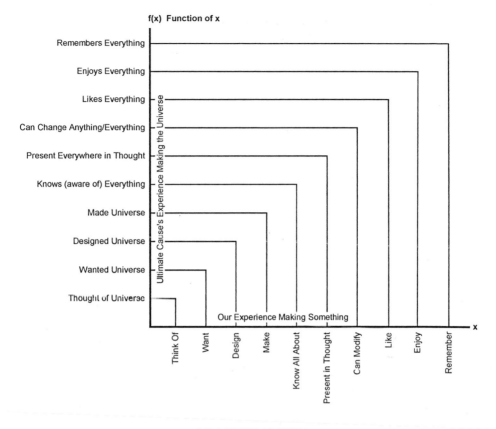

PRACTICALITY

Evidence of the practicality of Ultimate Cause is that the people of the United States of America have used it as the philosophical base for the most prosperous life mankind has achieved. The structure of the governmental, social institutions, ideals and values are based on the idea of Ultimate Cause. UC is the basis for the ideas that all men are equal to the government, separation of church and state, the people are responsible for morality and ethics. Morality and ethics are debated and established by law. The justice system is to provide for the safety of the people, provide restitution, and habituation of offenders. Those who think in terms of Ultimate Cause have personal tranquility and foster social harmony. They view things objectively. Under them, the sciences are free to develop understanding of the universe, develop technology, and provide resources for a more abundant life.

B said, "Each person decides whether a thing is proven to him or her. Proof is individual and personal."

For more on proof, see APPENDIX 5.

B 5
ON FAILURE

After some reflection, B continued. "There is something you haven't touched on much. It is the matter of failure in life. You know we all face termination. We all weaken and die if we don't have a fatal accident. Failure is doing things that turn out wrong. You do things and they offend people. You work on a job and it is a failure. Everyone connected with it looks at it as a disaster. There are little personal things and then there are public things that many people know about. How does the idea of Ultimate Cause help?"

I said, "Certainly. This is a valuable part of the idea of C. For UC there is no failure. C views our lives as a drama. We, too, can see the drama of our failure. Failure gives meaning to life. Without failure and mortality there is no struggle, effort, no success. In the case of Jesus, it led to pain, suffering, and death on the cross. We have our miseries.

"You know the games we play. They are little slices of life. Only one person or team wins. Everyone else fails. And even on the way to championship, there are failures. Football teams seldom have a perfect season. And even if they do, they don't win the championship every season.

"We play games to test ourselves to see who we are in comparison to others, to taste success and to experience failure, the drama of failure.

"Thinking about C during our failures gives us perspective. We are participating in the processes. No matter how successful we are, eventually we die. And what we have accomplished is replaced, if not replace long before we die.

"I have seen new buildings. They were great achievements. Then, I have lived long enough to see them become the old buildings. I have seen them torn down for new buildings. Then I have seen them become old and replaced. I have seen positions filled by a series of people. Success or failure, the drama goes on. We remember and UC remembers. I remember something of my grandparents, quite a lot about my parents, relatives, and communities in which I lived. UC remembers it all. After all is said and done, memories remain. UC remembers it all"

III

PRACTICE
KNOW YOURSELF

THINKING LIKE ULTIMATE CAUSE

HOW TO THINK OF ULTIMATE CAUSE

Thoughts about UC go through my mind many times a day. They flicker to consciousness. I think, "There was nothing. There was no universe, no stars, no sun, no earth, no atoms, no subatomic particle, no molecules, no cells, no life, no energy, no people, not anything. C thought about and wanted a universe with galaxies of stars, atoms, subatomic particles, life, people, processes,---.

"C started the development of the universe. C caused the universe to come into being. C started the development of galaxies of stars. They increased to billions of galaxies, each with billions of stars. They expanded to being millions of light years apart.

"That universe continues on and on into space, beyond our ability to gather light. Here is our sun, earth, oceans, land, mountains, trees, grass, animals, people, cultures ---. I contemplate. I think about the greater universe, the micro-universe, living things, people, cultures, history, anthropology. C caused the universe to come into being. Things do not cause themselves.

"C likes and experiences everything. C remembers everything. C is beyond the universe. Yet C is aware of everything in the universe. C envelops the universe by something like thought, awareness. C likes and enjoys each thing, creature, and person. C enjoys each one as though he, she, or it is the only thing, creature, or person."

I think of experiencing with C everything I think, say, feel and do. I think of places and people I have known: carpenter boy in Nazareth;

73

Karnack temple with inscription on the wall of a king watching mutilation of captives with their parts in a pile; the huge elephant in temple grounds in Sangli, India; lady in rags asleep with baby in park at Delhi; on Yangtze riverboat young people knowing the meaning of abstract; volcano in Hawaii; dog teams in Alaska; Pribilof Island seals and foxes; boys playing soccer along the Amazon; lady fixing dinner on house on stilts; senator drunk being led of the Senate floor in Washington as he was telling about how bills were drafted; President Roosevelt driving up mall guards on every street corner; thunder hole in Maine; baby skunks in wheat field of Kansas; blue birds with green worms to feed babies; crowds at football games; Edinburgh Castle; Paris; experiences of a lifetime that go on and on—

As I think of people's circumstances, I remember, "C thinks of them as I do. C knows them better than I do. C through me saw the people at Luxor, Egypt sitting in the shade of a tree surrounded by goats in the swirling dust. C saw through me in India the people in the bazaars."

C sees and experiences the complete life of everyone. C is aware of everything I think and do. C knows more about me than I do of myself. C is my buddy, my complete confidant. C enjoys me. So I should enjoy living and enjoy knowing as much about our world and universe as possible.

When I see things I don't like, when I see people doing things of which I do not approve, I think, "C is enjoying them. I should too." It is all part of the drama.

I am impressed by the compression of information in computers, eggs, sperm, pollen, DNA ---. We are just beginning to know about these things. C designed and put the processes into operation billions of years ago when the universe began. Perhaps the universe started as a particle (something like a cell with something like DNA and RNA) with all the instructions for the development of the universe with the earth, the people and all the many cultures, like the original cell from which each of us developed. So the universe may have developed automatically to be as it is, from the instructions in the original single cell egg that was the start of the whole universe.

C, along with me, experiences and enjoys everything I see, hear, taste, smell, feel, and think. It is the same with everyone.

C is my companion. C remembers everything, my every thought and feeling. C has them in memory beyond the existence of the universe. C has more and better memory than all the computers and recorders of the world. There is nothing in the universe as great as C. I know C beyond a reasonable doubt. I have rational confidence in UC. You can too.

I think of C as greater than the greatest person imaginable. C knows my every thought and feeling. C understands me completely. C is recording my whole life beyond the existence of the universe. C is doing the same with every person. I think of C as abstract abilities. UC is more than a person. UC designed people to develop. The design provides for the development of all the various people of the earth.

We think about C in terms of our experiences. We have no other way. C wanted, designed, made, is aware of everything. C likes, experiences, enjoys, and remembers everything about the universe. I think of C as my companion, experiencing everything with me. C made the universe processes so all these things come to pass automatically without C's intervention. Yet C may intervene at any time, in any way. C is present everywhere, is aware of everything.

THINK LIKE UC

We can think somewhat like UC thinks of the universe.

THINK OF YOURSELF BEING ULTIMATE CAUSE

Think of the universe as you know it. There is the greater universe of billions of galaxies with billions of stars in each. The sun is one of the stars. The earth is a big round ball of rock, water, earth, plants, animals, and people with wonderful cultures.

The earth is a ball revolving in space with the sun. Everything is made up of small electrical particles relating to each other by rules to make atoms, molecules, cells of life, people, galaxies of stars. There are the laws of organization and relationships – gravity, centrifugal force, magnetism, osmosis, photosynthesis, thermodynamics, all the systems of rain, evaporation. There are grazers and predators — the processes of life, pollen, eggs and sperm, creatures developing, growing, maturing, reproducing, declining, dying, being recycled. There is DNA, RNA, compression of instruction for the development of whole creatures in a single cell smaller than a pinhead, mutations to make new creatures so there are all the different forms of life.

Think of all the things people have and are doing. Think of the roads, cars, great buildings, telephone lines, power lines, wireless communication, and all the cultures of the people. I see boys and girls playing, people singing and dancing, limping along. I see people looking at the hills, the mountains covered with trees, the ocean waves splashing on the sandy beaches and rocky cliffs. People are building, planting, harvesting, painting. People are being born, are becoming sick, feeling pain, suffering, dying. People are learning the natural laws. They are making wonderful machines. They have computers. They are going to the moon and back. They are developing moral and ethical rules. They are learning to care for each other and their environment. They are learning to enjoy the universe. They are learning how to have personal tranquility and social harmony. They are learning to know me, Ultimate Cause. It is all processes. It goes on and on. I observe and remember it all. (Remember I am thinking like I am C). It is just like I want it. There are processes of development toward complexity and intelligence. I am enjoying experiences with each person, his or her unique life.

I caused all this. It all exists at my will. It is a great display. It is a great show. I can do anything with it I want. I like it. I enjoy it. I remember everything.

You have thought one way C thinks of the universe.

Think of all the things you know about the universe, from the galaxies of stars to the subatomic particles, the things you know about chemistry, physics, geology, anthropology, mathematics, psychology, sociology, families, business, the people of the world, all the cultures. Then think of UC having experienced all those things with you, through you, with every other person on earth and independently as Ultimate Cause; and having it all in memory beyond the existence or the universe. This is your companion and mine.

SUMMARY

We rationally know Ultimate Cause of the universe that we symbolize with C, UC (or any other symbol). We know UC without a reasonable doubt. We accept the rationality of the universe. The universe is understandable, logical. We accept the reliability of cause and effect. There is cause of the universe. C is objectively separate, different from the universe. We think of C as abstract, not like the universe or part of the universe. The whole universe is processes. C is not an "a", "the", "it", "she", "he", "thing", "being."

C has in concept all the qualities and abilities of mankind and more. C designed, made it all continuing processes, including us. We are increasing our knowledge of the greater universe as we study astronomy. We are increasing our knowledge of the micro-universe as we study physics, chemistry, and genetics.

C is aware of everything in the universe, able to change anything, everything. C experiences with each person every thought and feeling and preserves it all in constant awareness memory beyond the existence of the universe. The purpose of our being is for C to experience our unique lives. We can think of C as our buddy experiencing with each of us our pleasures, successes, victories, pains, miseries, defeats, sorrows, death.

We can think of the world as a stage on which we are players. We play for C. C likes and enjoys every player, every act. We can enjoy the play along with C. We also interact with each other. We enjoy the play. We see the wonderful parts people are playing. The tragedies are important, as are the farces, comedies, love stories, heroic acts, tragedies, and pending disasters. There are new actors coming on all around us.

We can share with C an objective view of ourselves and the world. We can talk to C in our thoughts and think of C's logical response. We need to have a framework of ideas in our minds to think C's responses. Any moment, you can think of C. C with you and through you is seeing, thinking about, experiencing the thing you are.

THOUGHTS

A PARABLE OF OUR SITUATION

On TV, there have been series about survivors. One was on an island. Sixteen people were put on the island; presumably "marooned." Camera crews recorded what they said and did night and day. People were eliminated by voting, until finally there was one final survivor. Of course, then even the last one left, so none was left. I see the story as a parable of our situation as people on the earth.

Notice mortality. They came to the island and left. Representing our coming to the earth and leaving. Second, notice the alliance. The last survivor continued because of the alliance he made with others. We need others to survive. We survive longer when we work together. Third, notice the recording is preserved and played. This represents UC knowing and preserving it in memory outside and beyond the existence of the universe.

In a million years or a few million years, there probably won't be any people on earth. UC will still be experiencing the earth and the universe. Apparently, much of the life of the earth changes about every 160-360 million years or so. It is said the saber-toothed tiger of many years ago is not related to modern tigers. New species develop. Perhaps in millions of years, the processes could develop new intelligent beings something like us but not related to us.

MODELS

Our thoughts are models. We think in terms of models. We constantly make and remake them. Our minds are virtual realities of our surroundings. The virtual reality of our minds varies with our perspective. Scientists make equations and models so we can think of and work with them. A lot of equations are used in the modeling involved in spaceships going to the moon and coming back.

KINDRED SPIRITS

Jesus is a kindred spirit, our brother, as are Socrates, John Calvin, Martin Luther, Einstein, Muhammad, Buddha, and many others. They had great insight. Records tell us what they thought. We can think as they did. We have more information, and so we can think beyond them. Every generation has more knowledge.

Jesus shows us many things about UC. He used the terms of his day. He used the term "heavenly Father." Jesus said my heavenly Father is in me and I in Him. This is saying UC is aware of my every thought and feeling so, in this sense I am in UC. I am aware of some of UC's thoughts, so UC is in me. Jesus shows us that C shares our pain, suffering, and death as he suffered and died on the cross.

ULTIMATE CAUSE AND VIRTUAL REALITY

We may think of UC as something like thought. In thought, we are anyplace we think about. UC's thought includes everything in the universe. So UC is everywhere in something like thought and awareness. Thought is virtual reality. In each of our minds are maps, pictures of the world and universe. It is so accurate, we can thread a needle.

We think of UC having something like thought, something like virtual reality of the universe before starting it and UC has something like virtual reality of us and the whole universe as it continues to develop. Many times a day I think of UC seeing and thinking of the things I am seeing and thinking. I think of UC enjoying it with me and through me.

CHECK UP

DO YOU HAVE THE BENEFITS OF KNOWING UC?

ASK YOURSELF

Affirming these statements indicates that you have the values of knowing Ultimate Cause.

UC is more than a passing diversion idea for me.
UC was before the universe existed.
I think of UC in human terms, but know UC is abstract, not part of the universe.
UC caused all the traits we have, so has them, in "mind."
UC caused the universe to be as it is, all processes.
UC thinks my thoughts with me.
UC has all my thoughts. I have some of UC's thoughts.
Mentally, we are in each other, when we have the same thoughts..
I think objectively some of the time.
I am important to UC.
I think of UC as my companion.
UC likes and enjoys me and everyone.
I think of my whole life of thoughts and feelings preserved in UC's memory.
UC does not judge us, but made us mortal, so we need morality and ethics.

I accept rationality, cause and effect, processes, objectivity, abstract, mortality, experience, science, the universe, cause of the universe, and myself.

I know there is more than earthly goals.

Our lives are important beyond the universe.

Even if I have nothing, achieve no goals, I know I am important to UC. I am unique.

Wars, inhumanity of man to man, and genocide are moral and ethical problems for us to solve.

Things are as they are because UC made them so they could develop to be as they are.

I have real joy in thinking of UC.

I like to think of UC enjoying the universe with me.

I like to think of UC enjoying the universe before I was here.

I like to think of UC enjoying the universe after I am no longer alive on earth.

Everything now makes sense. I am not bored, discouraged, lonely, enraged, perplexed.

I realize I had many of these ideas subconsciously. Now I consciously think of them.

I notice everything on the earth is mortal. All achievements are replaced. So I look to C for permanence.

C preserves it all in memory. It is up to C if there is more for us.

I always have something interesting to think about.

The whole universe is dynamic, changing, mortal.

Why are we here? What is the purpose of our being?
The purpose of our being is for C to experience with each person his or her unique thoughts and feelings.

What happens to us eventually?
Our whole lives of thoughts, words, feelings, and actions are preserved beyond the existence of the universe in C's memory.

What is our job in living?
Our job in living is to understand all we can about the universe and C. It is to make living as good as we can for ourselves and all other people. It is to wisely care for the earth.

There is the possibility that the universe is part of a completely automatic system developing from something like DNA in the original particle of the universe. Things are as they are. It is all processes of development. UC is experiencing it all.

I think about UC because of my background. Thoughts about C came to me without intention. You and I can, by intention, think about UC. You probably have thought about C, but may have used other symbols.

Ultimate Cause made the universe as it is. It is processes, development, decay, recycling, with development toward complexity and intelligence.

Ultimate Cause likes and enjoys everything about the universe. We can too.

We know Ultimate Cause when we accept; the discoveries of the scientific method, that the universe is rational, cause and effect, the universe is processes, objectivity, the abstract, and inferring UC from our knowledge of the universe.

The purpose of this book is to provide a view agreeable to people of all cultures, so everyone can know Ultimate Cause. Those who know Ultimate Cause have personal tranquility and foster social harmony.

You have the complete framework for your philosophy, from the beginning to the end. You have a lifetime to fill in the pieces of the drama. You will fill in scientific knowledge. You will further moral knowledge and practices, care for the earth, care for people. You will learn more about Ultimate Cause, UC's participation in the universe, and perhaps more about what is beyond the universe. You will never forget Ultimate Cause. You know C without any doubt.

To UC, everything is as interesting and beautiful as we do our greatest experiences, fondest dreams.

What does UC think about the gods?

UC enjoys the gods, and all peoples' thoughts about them. C enjoys every thought of every person.

I hope the idea of Ultimate Cause has become living thought in your mind.

JUDGMENT

C likes everything about the universe. C does not judge anyone. C unconditionally accepts us. Due to our mortality, we have to judge. We have to decide what is beneficial for our survival and what is detrimental. To survive as long and well as we can, we avoid and/or eliminate the detrimental. We nurture the moral and ethical. We protect individual lives and society as a whole. This we do to survive as long and as well as we can, individually, as people and cultures.

JUSTICE

The goal of justice is social harmony and personal tranquility. It should not involve revenge. It should include prevention, restitution, and rehabilitation where possible. Punishment should be involved only when it contributes to prevention of disruption and/or contributes to tranquility and harmony.

WISDOM

Wisdom is to know Ultimate Cause. To know Ultimate Cause, one needs to accept: rationality, cause and effect, that the universe is processes, objective thinking, thinking of the abstract, mortality and moral responsibility.

I smile to myself when I think about the wonderful universe with all the variety of people and their activities. I smile to myself when I think about UC enjoying the universe and people of the world. I smile to myself when I think of UC observing me enjoying the universe and people. I smile to myself when I think of UC enjoying the world when I am gone, as UC did before I was here. I smile to myself when I think of my being in UC's memory beyond the existence of the universe. I smile to myself when I think of myself, part of the universe able to think of the universe and its cause.

UC designed the natural laws and set them into operation to cause the development of the vast universe of galaxies and the intricate structure of the micro-universe of subatomic particles, energy, gravity, magnetic fields, DNA, human life, and cultures.

C is everywhere aware. C has me and you in full focus. You and I have C's full attention. C knows everything about us. There is nothing more to know about us than C knows. I find knowing C is aware of me all the time is comforting and exciting, and gives meaning to my life. I know C is enjoying with me, everything I see, hear, feel, taste, smell, touch, and think.

It amuses me and makes me smile to myself when I think of C enjoying with me and through me. I am part of C's "thought." I am in C's virtual reality. So are you.

BRIEF

We infer UC from our knowledge of the universe. The red shift in the spectrum of light from galaxies indicates our universe is expanding. An expanding universe means it was small to the point of not being. A beginning means a cause outside of the universe. Cause of the universe is not a phenomenon for which we can seek a cause, so is Ultimate Cause. We infer the properties of UC from our experiences. When we make something, we want it. We design it. We make it. In our thoughts, we are present in it and know all abaut it. We enjoy it. We experience it. We remember it.

We infer that UC would have at least our abilities and our experiences making things, as UC causes the universe

MAKING SENSE

The only explanation of the universe that makes sense to me is that it is a drama for Ultimate Cause.

NO MATTER WHO YOU ARE

UC likes and enjoys you, no matter what the circumstances of your life. UC is experiencing your life with you. UC has you in full focus and in memory. UC sees your life is interesting and unique. UC enjoys you wherever you are, as much in the desert, the swamp, along a river, in the Arctic, inner city, isolated, in a crowd, rich or poor, in prison, castle, mansion, homeless, in space. UC enjoys your life with you, whatever your sex, sexual orientation, sex life, occupation, age, health, race, family, disfigurement, mental ability, mental development, your unique thoughts, passions, zeal, fears, hates, loves, actions, projects, work; regardless of what you have done or are doing, regardless of crimes, brutalities, terrorism, genocide, perpetrator, victim,---.

FREEDOM

You are free when your life is not threatened, your mind is not restrained, access to information is not limited, your habits and beliefs do not limit your thinking, and you can think logically.

Four freedoms have been mentioned: freedom of speech, of religion, from fear, from want.

One is free in thought and rich in mind, thinking about Ultimate Cause even when one is without anything, in any circumstance.

Epictetus is an example of objectivity and freedom of mind. His mind was above his physical situation. While his master twisted his leg, he objectively said, "If you keep twisting, it will break."

YOU NOW KNOW UC

Now you know Ultimate Cause that designed and made the universe ongoing processes as it is. UC likes and enjoys everything about the universe, including every person. UC is aware of everything, including every person's thoughts and feelings. UC holds in memory outside the universe every person's thoughts, feelings, words, and deeds. Our whole lives are in UC's memory beyond the universe.

You know UC is your companion. UC has you in full focus. You can now see the universe as UC does. You now like and enjoy everything about the universe as UC does. You know we are responsible for making life good for every person. The only view that makes sense of the life of man, the world and the universe is Shakespeare's "All the world's a stage." Add to it that we play for Ultimate Cause, ourselves, and to each other.

Something like thought is the ultimate reality. Jesus indicates the primacy of thought. (Matthew 9:22)— "Your faith has made you whole." (Proverbs 23:7)— "As he thinketh in his heart, so is he." (Ephesians 2:8)— "You are saved by faith."

We are in C's memory now. We have C's complete attention. C's attention is completely focused on each of us. There is nothing more to know about each of us than C knows and has in memory. What more C may have for us is up to C.

Each person has a complete life at every moment. One does not need to live long to have a complete life.

Now you know Ultimate Cause. You are in a long line of people who have thought of Ultimate Cause: Thomas Jefferson, Erasmus

Darwin, St. Augustine, Jesus, the Psalmist, Moses, and the countless people for whom we have no record. A small part of what has happened and thought is recorded, a smaller part of it remains, and a smaller part of it is known by us.

Consider that each person has a thought about every six seconds we are awake. Consider that there are six or so billion people in the world. There are trillions of thoughts. And C knows them all. We are part of an immense universe. Ultimate Cause knows it all. UC is capable of this. We know Ultimate Cause. You and I are part of the drama and are permitted to be observers.

MONK

As we were sitting and contemplating, there was sort of swish at the door. It opened a crack and an eye was seen peering in; the door opened and there stood Monk. He wore the habit that he could make look like a suit or a jacket, depending on the way he wore it.

Now Monk was a real monk. He had spent his life traveling the world to know and experience every way of life. Monk was always on the move while staying long enough to be comfortable with the language and get the mental set and spirit of the people. He had spent time in Rome exploring the archives. He had been a monk in Tibet, made the treks of Hindus, been to Mecca, spent time with tribes on the Amazon, with the Pygmies of Africa, the Aborigines of Australia, the Inuit of Greenland, with the conservative Jews in Jerusalem. He had studied at Harvard, Yale, Stanford, MIT, Cal Tech, Oxford, Cambridge, and the Sorbonne.

Here was wisdom itself. He was a presence wherever he went. He had the presence of a Lama. We had bumped into him several times. I had met him on a cruise around South America. That was the first time I recognized who he was. He was then on his retirement cruise as a priest. He had been an acting bishop at one time, but didn't want to be a bishop. He sat at our table on the cruise. I asked him to bless me. He did and asked me, "Do you feel better?" He was on a flight back from the Amazon. Only briefly did he tell a little of spending a year living with tribal people along the Amazon River in Peru. On a cruise on the Yangtze River, he was a member of a small group on a tour of China with local professors as special guides. I spoke to him only briefly. He gave me a way of contacting him. I haven't.

He had a small computer with a monitor on one of the lenses of his glasses. He seemed to show up everywhere. I felt myself fortunate to have had brief conversations. He had interesting observations. I blame myself for not having really explored the depths of his thinking. But then, who can know the depths of another person's thinking? I just don't know how to get people to open up. I did get him to open up once as I met him on a walk. He told me about being an AFEES in Europe during the Second World War. As a downed member of the air force, he evaded, escaped, and survived. He had worked with the underground.

I felt fortunate that he would come by to see me. Here he was at a time when he could share his insights with some of my friends. He looked at me with a look that impelled me to explain the gathering. That I did briefly and he understood. He was used to grasping the situation.

He said, "People all over the earth are thinking of cause of the universe, in terms of their own languages and culture. They are beginning to see that mortality is the basis of morality, and UC is not mortal, so not moral. They are seeing that morality is our problem and we had better get at it or we are in for a lot more difficulty than we need to have.

"I do not know of anyone consciously inferring UC from their knowledge of the universe as you are. Although, of course, Ultimate Cause has always been in people's subconscious as they think of God.

"Well, you have the problem of presenting UC in such a way that people will know UC is their companion and in that companionship feel common companionship with all the people of the world. That is a tall order. I think one problem is objectivity. People all over the world are self-absorbed, concentrating on themselves. Of course, this is natural. Everyone has to make a living. Everyone has the heritage of the struggle to survive. Everyone holds on to whatever they think makes them secure.

"On the other hand, there is this Vision thing. People hope. They are always seeking more. They are asking, 'What can we do to make things better, without losing what we have?'

"Now, the idea of Ultimate Cause of the universe is an idea of hope. In knowing UC, people have the vision of companionship with UC and with all the people of the world. We have the vision of being in UC's memory beyond the existence of the universe; the vision of personal tranquility, social harmony; the vision of a unified view of religion, science, and philosophy; the vision of social structures that serve all mankind to provide the best possible life for every person on earth; the vision of peace on earth and goodwill among men. This hope involves many people knowing UC. This hope is to eliminate violent enforcement of God-given morality. This hope is that everyone will treat everyone as equals because they are fellow companions of UC that likes and enjoys everyone equally, completely. So slavery is eliminated. Members of religious organizations treat non-members the same as members.

"The idea of moral, providential God has served mankind with faith and hope, but is not adequate for people with the knowledge of our time. The idea of God has been developing over the history of man's existence. It continues to develop toward the idea of Ultimate Cause of the universe that caused the universe to operate by what we call natural laws.

DEVELOLPMENT OF THE IDEA OF GOD

"You may have noticed the development of the idea of God from the personal, local God of Abraham, Isaac, and Jacob, to Jacob seeing God present in places other than his home and interested in all the families of the earth. But God was still the family, tribal God. Through his family, all the families of the earth would be blessed. His family would be blessed with expansion and prosperity."

Genesis 28:10-16 says:
"And Jacob went out from Beersheba, and went toward Haran.--- and he took stones of the place, and put them for his pillows, and lay down in that place to sleep. And he dreamed, and behold a ladder set up on the earth, and the top of it reached to heaven: and behold the angels of God ascending and descending on it. And, behold, the Lord stood above it, and said I am the Lord God of Abraham thy father, and the God of Isaac: the land whereon you lie, to you will I give it, and to thy seed; And they shall be as the dust of the earth: and thou shalt spread abroad to the west, and to the east, and to the north, and to the south: and in thee and in thy seed shall all the families of the earth be blessed. – And Jacob awaked out of his sleep, and he said, "Surely the Lord is in this place; and I knew it not."

Monk continued his observations, "The Lord God of Abraham, Isaac, and Jacob was a personal, family, local God. But in this experience, Jacob changed his idea of God. Jacob now saw God was in other places than his home territory.

"Notice the definition of God in the dictionary of 1952 and the more recent dictionary of 1998.

The New Webster Encyclopedia Dictionary of the English Language, 1952 defines God:
"god--- A being conceived of as possessing divine power, and therefore, to be propitiated by sacrifice, worship, and the like: a divinity; the Supreme Being; Jehovah: the eternal Spirit, the Creator, and the Sovereign of the universe: any person or thing exalted too much in estimation, or deified and honored as the chief good."

Merriam Webster's Collegiate Dictionary 1998 gives this:
"god — 1 capitalized: the supreme or ultimate reality: as a. the Being perfect in power, wisdom, and goodness who is worshipped as creator and ruler of the universe b. Christian Science: the incorporeal divine Principle ruling over all as eternal Spirit: infinite mind. 2: a being or object believed to have more than natural attributes and powers and to require human worship; specifically: one controlling a particular aspect or part of reality

3: a person or thing of supreme value."

"We notice that Jesus used both the designation God and heavenly Father. Jesus in healing the woman of Canaan changed from the thought that he had been sent only to the lost sheep of Israel. Matthew 15:22-28.

"Peter changed his idea about God when being told by the voice from heaven 'What God has cleansed call not thou common.' The Holy Spirit fell on the Gentiles. Peter realized that God accepts other than people of Israel. And the people, he told about the experience changed their ideas about God. Acts 11:6-18.

"People are constantly changing from one view of God to another.

"Notice that today some Christians say God is God of everyone, but not included in providence, unless they confess, acknowledge God as a Christian, as they see Christianity. The same is true of Islam. One has to be a member of Islam or is not right in Allah's view. The same is true of other religions.

"The idea of God does change. It has changed and is changing. So it is possible for God to be thought of as cause of the universe, Ultimate Cause. Many people today are thinking this way whether they use the designation UC or not.

"When religions accept the idea of Ultimate Cause, ritual in church services, study groups, meditations, prayers—will be educational. They will be about knowing more about the universe, about logic, thinking rationally, human values, morality that fits the way people are, psychology, sociology, cultures, personal tranquility, social harmony— all about knowing the universe and inferring UC from that knowledge. Religions will become educational, continuing education. They will continue to be a vital part of the culture. Churches will provide resources to help people know the universe and Ultimate Cause. Churches will provide fellowship for people aware of their shared companions with UC. Churches will foster social structures that provide services that meet the needs of mankind, so everyone has as good a life as possible.

"The difficulty with defining Ultimate Cause as God is that people may say, 'UC is just God. I already know God.' Thomas Aquinas in effect did this when after he proved the existence of first cause, he said, 'This everyone calls God.'

"On the other hand, the idea of God is becoming Ultimate Cause in many people's minds. I heard a Roman Catholic who said he had never been to a Protestant service say, 'I don't believe in the devil'. I hear a lot of people say that. I hear people say, 'If there is a hell, it is what you experience on earth, in this life.' People are debating morality. They are trying to develop the natural moral laws.

"The idea of revealed God has brought peace to some people, but has not provided universal peace. Revealed gods are being invoked in conflicts. Even within groups, there is conflict over interpretation of the records of revelations. Ultimate Cause is what we infer from our knowledge of the way things are. It will take a lot of work to get everyone to have a common understanding of the universe from which we infer UC.

"Ultimate Cause is the rational view of God. Religions can accept the idea of UC. Knowledge of nature has been the foundation of religion since the beginning of human thought. But mankind has intellectually known little about the universe till recently. With the development of philosophy and the sciences, people are able to develop a view of the universe from which they can infer cause of the universe as capability to cause the universe to be as it is.

"Some of the amazing feats of Joseph and Moses in Egypt can be attributed to their observations and knowledge of nature. Thomas Aquinas writes that he agrees with St. Paul that by natural powers of reasoning, we can know that God exists. Aquinas calls this first cause, which is cause of the universe, God.

"Thomas Aquinas agrees with St. Augustine that 'God —is sufficiently almighty—to bring good even from evil.' This is similar to UC seeing the mortal life of man (elements of which people call evil) a drama to experience.

"John Davis in his *Dictionary of the Bible* reflects the thought of many when he writes,

"*This primary idea of God, in which is summed up what is known as theism, is the product of that general revelation, which God makes of himself to all men, on the plane of nature. The truths involved in it are continually reiterated, enriched, and deepened in the Scriptures; but they are not so much revealed in them as presupposed at the foundation of the special revelation -- On the plane of nature men can learn only what God necessarily is---.*"

"This indicates that people of that time, before and after 1920, were thinking that knowledge of nature is presupposed at the foundation of belief in the idea of God. This puts Ultimate Cause of nature as the foundation of the idea of God.

"The foundation of the idea of God (Ultimate Cause of nature) has been neglected.

"Luther longed to know God accurately where he is most himself, (which is the universe). (Kerr p.29)

"Luther did not know the universe well enough to infer UC. We are fortunate to know the universe with tools.

"John Calvin says 'God is first manifested—in the structure of the world –simply as the Creator—' (Kerr p. 5)

"One can notice the similarity to Ultimate Cause known by inference from knowledge of the structure of the universe.

"Religions contribute traditional views of morality, rituals, meditations, continuing education about the universe, and rational thought to knowing UC. They can be communities of fellowship for those who know their common companionship with UC. Churches can be centers of fellowship and education that bring the people of the world together so everyone feels companionship with every other person.

"To sum up, the best we can do is think about and study Ultimate Cause and encourage others to do the same. Those who understand and think in terms of UC are enjoying the companionship with UC and all other people, whether they think in terms of UC or not. For we know UC is everyone's companion. All any person needs to do to know UC is: to know about the universe and logically infer UC from that knowledge. UC will live in people's minds to the extent they want to know UC, accept knowledge of the universe, and infer its cause.

"It seems to me that the time is right for your book about Ultimate Cause. It seems the time is right for people to bring their subconscious awareness of UC to conscious thought about Ultimate Cause as their most intimate companion preserving every person's total life of thoughts, feelings, words and actions in memory beyond the existence of the universe"

Monk paused and there was silence.

CONCLUSION

THE GAME

My friend said, "Let's look at it as a game. The game is to answer the questions: Why are we here? What is going to happen to us? What is our life all about?

"You start out with our situation. We are in a universe that we know by our everyday observations, the systematic observations we call the sciences, revelations of religions, and reasoning that we call philosophy. These we have to work with.

"You say, let's think of the universe as a big box. Outside the box is cause of the box (universe). Cause of the box is adequate to cause the box (universe) to be as it is. The answers to our questions are in knowing cause of the universe, which we can only know in terms of our experience. When we make something, we think about it, want it, design, cause its development, know all about it, use, enjoy, and remember all about it. In our terms, cause of the universe would have such experience causing the universe.

"We make things because we need them, to use them or just to enjoy and experience them. We know of no reason cause of the universe would need the universe, so we conclude that cause of the universe caused the universe to experience and enjoy it. That explains why we are here and what our lives are all about. We are here for cause of the universe to experience and enjoy. Cause of the universe knows all about us, even our every thought, feeling, word, and deed, remembers it all beyond the existence of the universe. Cause of the universe is our most intimate companion experiencing with us our every thought and feeling.

"Since cause of the universe knows our every thought and feeling, we can communicate with cause of the universe with our thoughts. And we can think of the response of cause of the universe by our knowledge of the universe.

"The whole of our lives, every thought, feeling, word and deed is in cause of the universe beyond the existence of the universe. The concept of cause of the universe is so simple, most everyone has had it. Yet no one, to our knowledge, has developed the idea, so they think to cause of the universe, think the answer of cause of the universe from their knowledge of the universe, have personal tranquility and think of everyone as their companion in our mutual companionship with cause of the universe."

I responded, "Great. That is it."

At this point, B piped up. "You know, I notice there has been no mention of a mystical relationship with Ultimate Cause. UC is known in pure rational terms. We think of UC with our eyes wide open looking at the universe. We learn to see it as UC does. Mathematicians see elegance in their solutions of problems. Scientists see beauty in the models they make of the universe and its parts. Ultimate Cause is an elegant beautiful model of cause of the universe. I have to run. It has been fun being in on the gang."

Gradually everyone left after the regular chitchat.

When my friend had left, I said to Ultimate Cause, "Well, C, there it is. What is going to come of this?"

C said in my mind (I thought C's answer), "Well, I have seen it all from before the beginning. I know it all, have experienced it all. It is a great show. You would think it a great show if you had made it. Wouldn't you? I made it so you have a time on earth. And there will be an end to man's life on earth besides the end of your life on earth. You don't know how it all will come out. Just enjoy the ride. I will think of something."

I can think of no greater companion than the one who thought of a universe, designed it, had it made, knows all about it, from the farthest galaxy to the smallest subatomic particles, from the simplest life forms to human cultures, knows my every thought and feeling from my beginning and knows what is beyond the universe. The greatest thought anyone can have is that Ultimate Cause of the universe is my companion and yours.

You may ignore cause and effect. You may forget about Ultimate Cause. They are not going away.

IV

APPENDICES

APPENDIX 1
THE SEARCH FOR ULTIMATE CAUSE

Philosophy has been described as the search for ultimate cause by reasoning from knowledge of the universe.

Science searches for Ultimate Cause by the scientific method.

Religions seek to know Ultimate Cause by revelations, dreams, feelings, inspirations, experience.

Philosophy, science, and religion are united in seeking to know Ultimate Cause. They are united in contributing to knowing Ultimate Cause. They are united in knowing Ultimate Cause. Each has its part to play.

Religions bring imagination, art, experiences and tradition to the idea of UC. The sciences provide better and better views of the universe from which to infer UC. Philosophy analyzes and questions to make clear the idea of Ultimate Cause.

The sciences give us descriptive models of the universe that are modified and verified by experimentation. The sciences require clear specific definitions. Models are used to describe, illustrate, and develop technologies and cosmology. They teach us to infer the properties of cause from our knowledge of phenomena. They help us think about the universe from which we infer Ultimate Cause.

Religions provide community, education, art, imagination, ritual, tradition, drama. They provide purpose for living. They involve emotion, feeling, faith, hope, conviction, love, and hate. They give meaning and enjoyment. They give us a vision of what Ultimate Cause may be and do.

Philosophers seek to know, analyze, speculate, coordinate, and provide logic and mathematics. They encourage us to be clear and specific about Ultimate Cause. Philosophy analyses how we know and advocate freedom of thought. Each (science, philosophy and religion) supplements the contribution of the others and helped us know Ultimate Cause.

APPENDIX 2
HOW TO THINK OF CAUSE OF THE UNIVERSE

An exercise:

Start out by thinking of the greatest person you can imagine. This person is aware of and knows everything about the universe from the farthest galaxies of stars to the smallest subatomic particles, from the smallest life forms to mankind. This person knows you intimately, every cell of your body, every thought and feeling. This person likes and enjoys you completely. This person is not limited by time or space. This person is everywhere in thought. This person can, by thought, change anything, everything in the universe. This person was before the universe existed and will be when the universe is no more. This person's attention is fully focused on you. This person shares your every thought and feeling. This person is your companion.

When you look out at the world and experience its beauty, when you experience pain and misery, think, "This person is experiencing this with me. This person enjoyed the world before I came and will when I am no longer here." We are in the great drama of the universe for and with this person.

Now go back and abstract the whole thing. Think of "this person" as cause of the universe, C. C is outside the universe. C is not part of the universe. C is my companion. C has all the qualities of a person and much more. C designed and caused the universe to develop so we are as we are. C is aware of everything in the universe. C is my companion.

This book is written to enable you to think about cause of the universe and have the point of view of cause of the universe. I hope there is enough repetition, so you practice thinking about UC in enough different settings, so UC automatically come into your mind, as UC comes into mine.

APPENDIX 3
MY EXPERIENCE

Experience 1

For eighty years, I have searched literature, philosophy, religion, and the sciences, and listened to wise men. I traveled, participated, and experienced. I sought to know as much as possible about the universe, the life of man, and what is beyond the universe.

I noticed that knowing the universe is an ongoing process. The tools of the sciences are enabling us to discover more and more about the greater universe of astrophysics, the subatomic particle structure of the universe, and processes.

I accept the logical discoveries reported by the sciences. One can verify that the universe is made up of galaxies of stars by using telescopes. One can verify that the galaxies are moving apart, that the universe is expanding by the red shift of the lines on spectrum of light that comes from the galaxies. This indicates there was a "before the universe." This indicates there is cause of the universe not the universe itself. The sciences enable us to know more about ourselves. We are learning about our bodies, genetics, our brains, and our minds. The humanities are growing. Due to technology, more people are living better, healthier, and longer.

I noticed that the one thing developing slowly is the idea of that which is beyond the universe. It seems to me that many people are little further along in thinking about what is beyond the universe than people were hundreds of years ago.

I am not satisfied with knowing about the universe and mankind. I am not satisfied participating in the life of the world, nor am I satisfied being part of our mortal universe. I want to know what is beyond the universe and have a part in it. Knowing UC satisfies me, and I hope it will you.

My whole life of thoughts, feelings, words and deeds is (as is yours) preserved in the Virtual Reality memory of UC beyond the existence of the universe. This is the capability of Ultimate Cause.

Experience 2

For every phenomenon, we seek a cause. So we seek cause of the phenomenon universe. We call the cause of the phenomenon universe C. I observe that everything is in process. So C caused the universe to be processes. I observe that things do not cause themselves. So C is separate from the universe. The universe is objective to C. C being separate from the universe, is not a phenomenon for which we can seek a cause. So C is Ultimate Cause.

We infer properties for the cause of phenomena. So from our knowledge of the universe, we infer properties of C. We can only know in human terms. We infer that in causing the universe C would have had experiences such as we have making things.

When we cause something, we start out thinking of it, wanting it. Then we design, make, know all about it, like it, enjoy and remember it. So we infer that C, something like: thought of, wanted, designed, made, knows all about, is in complete control of it, and remembers everything that happens in the universe. C knows all about us and has us in memory outside the universe.

UC is our companion, sharing every experience with us. When I see something I like or dislike, I think, "Ultimate Cause is seeing that through me and with me, as well as separate from me. UC likes and enjoys it. I should too. The time is coming when I will not be here to see these things. But UC will be seeing them and enjoying them as UC was before I came." I smile to myself thinking about Ultimate Cause enjoying the universe when I am no longer here.

President-elect George W. Bush, when he addressed the Texas legislature said, 'I will be back. I am going to Washington for a term of four or eight years.' This illustrates the attitude we should have about our lives. We are here for a term. It may be a few hours or many years. It is complete, whatever it turns out to be.

Experience 3

In my teens, in the 1930s, like other young people, I thought about the future. I wanted a great family, perhaps a fortune and a secure future for my descendants. I noticed that wars, revolutions, and unstable societies destroy people and security. Though I might have a great family and fortune, they would eventually be destroyed by unstable societies. What could I do to make the future secure, not only for my family, but all families, all people?

I decided that the important thing I should work for was stable social structures and peace among all people. But what could be done to get people to work together so everyone has a good life? Wars (conflicts, revolutions) develop from lack of socio-politico-economic stability. Dissatisfied people cause war, revolution. People without positive prospects make conflict. So I decided the primary goal was stable cultures. Cultures do not exist in isolation. So the goal of stability involves all cultures. Every person needs to see a way to have a full, satisfying life.

The only hope I saw of achieving security, peace, goodwill among all the people of the world was proclaimed at the birth of Jesus: "Glory to God in the highest and on earth peace goodwill among men." Christianity should bring peace and goodwill to all people. I decided to promote Christianity. I worked as a minister for forty years. Progress has been made. More people are living better than ever before.

Yet there is dissatisfaction, conflict, revolution, war, unemployment, hatred, fear. There is conflict among religions. Even among Christians, there is conflict. I keep asking myself, what is the difficulty? What is lacking? What is needed? Why is this not working? What would make peace and goodwill among all people? Then I remembered we are a great drama for Ultimate Cause. The drama is mankind developing from the simplest life form that merely metabolized, up to our present stage. The drama will go on as we struggle to develop culture that rationally cares for every person on earth.

I now see that peace can be achieved only by ideas. Without more and better thought, knowledge, and logic, mankind will have continual conflict. To attain peace, we must use our minds. We must live by our reasoning, rather than our instincts. We must learn how to establish and maintain stable world culture.

We are learning about the natural processes. We are learning to use them. We raise plants and animals. We make clothing and shelter. We extract minerals out of rocks. We manufacture chemicals, medicines, machines. We are learning to manipulate DNA. We are learning about ourselves. We are learning that peace and goodwill among men depend on everyone orienting their thoughts and action to cause of the universe.

So, I am pointing out a step in mankind's development of rationality. It is having Ultimate Cause as the base of our daily thought, philosophy, religion, science, politics, commerce. We analyze the world and universe to know it as it is. We order our lives and culture according to the way it is, as UC has caused it. I notice that revolutions, wars, and terrorism are promoted by intelligent, educated, powerful people. They have ideas that make for conflict. The idea of UC gives motivation for developing goodwill, peace, and brotherhood. Knowing UC brings tranquility and social harmony.

People have said they do not have time or energy to study the universe and think about UC. Anyone thinking this way is shortchanging himself or herself. Knowing Ultimate Cause is the most important thing one can do after providing the essentials of life. For thousands of years, people have thought one day in seven should be dedicated to thinking about the meaning of life, what is beyond the universe as they knew it, developing their culture, enjoying the arts and the relationships of community.

Experience 4

Having studied the problem for a lifetime of more than eighty years, I came to some conclusions. To have "peace on earth and goodwill among men" all the cultures of the world must be included. The way to peace and goodwill must be so desirable that everyone will want to participate. No one may be left out, since only a few people can destroy peace.

Every member of society must be provided satisfying opportunity. Justice is to protect society, habituate, and make restitution. Morality and ethics need to make the social structures serve every person on earth. Stable societies and governments operate on the basis of the equality of people. That means each person is to receive adequate services from the community. Services of the community include protecting property rights (in our present system). Those whose property is protected have the responsibility to use it for the welfare of all, and not let it harm other people or the environment. Property and wealth are not just to be personal possessions. They are to be used for the welfare of mankind. The community is to provide everyone as good a life as possible

It is my observation that the sustaining people of stable cultures function on the basis of the equality of mankind. This comes with the idea that Ultimate Cause enjoys everyone, and does not judge. Stable culture is possible with the idea of Ultimate Cause as the base for philosophy, science, and religion. UC likes and enjoys everyone and everything. We are to like and enjoy everyone. We are to provide for everyone. The universe and mankind operate by natural laws. We have discovered some of them, and we use them. We need to know more about them. We need to develop the natural laws of morality, psychology, sociology. We need to know what nature requires and live that way, so we can all live better.

APPENDIX 4
GOD

GOD COMPARED TO ULTIMATE CAUSE

Acts 7:40 Make us gods--.

Some people believe that God; personally, directly, immediately, and continually creates, maintains, and directs what is happening. God intervenes, is constantly, immediately, and providentially providing for each of his people. God makes revelations, gives commands, judges; punishes man for disobedience and rewards for obedience here or hereafter. God has opposition, is fighting evil, and enlists people in this conflict. God chooses some people to be his people, gives them land, and drives out people for them. God tells people to kill those who take their land. After this life, man continues to live in heaven or hell. People can avoid hell and go to heaven if they believe certain things (have faith), follow rituals, or are martyrs in Allah's conflict. Following ritual is important to God.

Ultimate Cause caused the universe to be as it is, considers it good, and enjoys it as a drama. UC has no opposition. UC likes and enjoys every part of the universe, including every person, regardless of circumstances or actions. The universe (including us) is developing, mortal, recycling. It operates automatically by processes. UC treats everyone alike.

We know UC in human terms (we have no other way) but UC is not part of the universe, is beyond the universe, and envelops the universe. UC observes every detail of the universe as a drama. UC is our intimate companion, sharing our every experience, thought, and feeling. Our whole lives are in UC's memory outside the universe. We can talk and laugh to UC and think UC's response from our knowledge of the universe. UC likes and enjoys us unconditionally, without judgment.

Ultimate Cause experiences with each person every thought, feeling, word, and deed. UC likes everyone. People think and talk to UC. People think UC's response from their knowledge of the universe. UC has something like virtual reality of every person's whole life beyond the universe. We know UC by inference from our knowledge of the universe. We know UC as capability to cause the universe (including the world and us) to be as we are. We are part of the recycling processes of the earth. We are mortal. We are moral in order to delay mortality; to live as well and long as we can. UC is not mortal. UC is not moral. Nothing is unfavorable to UC. Nothing is evil to UC. UC does not judge.

While shopping for cloth in a small Shop, the proprietor on being asked his nationality said, "I am a Jew from Israel." We high fived. I said, "I am writing a book about Ultimate Cause that knows our every thought and feeling." He immediate responded, "Some of them." This indicates an idea of God.

A well-educated lady, after reading a manuscript of this book, asked, "Is cause of the universe God?" Answer, "It depends on whether your idea of God is cause of the universe." She said, "I need to rethink my idea of the universe."

She is exactly right. Ultimate Cause is known by inference from your knowledge of the universe. The better our view of the universe, the better we know UC. A person's view of the universe determine his/her idea of its cause (whither God or Ultimate Cause).

There are two ideas about Elohim (God) in Genesis.

Genesis 1:1 - 2:3. (1) "In the beginning Elohim created the heavens and the earth. (1:21) And Elohim created the great sea animals and all that creeps, (having) a living soul, ---And Elohim saw that (it was) good."

Elohim made the heavens and earth as it is, as we know it, automatically operating by natural laws. Elohim sees it good and enjoys it. This idea is compatible with the idea of Ultimate Cause.

Genesis 2:4 - 3:24, (2:16) "—And Jehovah Elohim commanded the man saying. You may freely eat of every tree of the garden; but of the tree of knowledge of good and evil you may not eat, for in the day that you eat of it, dying you shall surely die. --- (3:6) and she took of its fruit and ate; and she also gave to her husband with her and he ate. And the eyes of both of them were opened, and they knew that they (were) naked. --- (3:14) and Jehovah Elohim said – (3:17) –to the man – Because you have listened to the voice of your wife and have eaten of the tree about which I commanded you, saying, You shall not eat from it, the ground shall be cursed because of you; --- (3:19) By the sweat of your face you shall eat bread until you return to the ground; for out of it you have been taken, for you are dust, and to dust you shall return."

From this has developed the idea that man is a sinner, rebelling against God

Here is the idea that knowledge is bad. It is better to be ignorant, (pure). Not knowing is purity.

Here is the idea that thinking in terms of good and evil causes difficulty. Think positively. People who think in terms of good and evil create difficulty, create evil.

As processes and natural laws are discovered and used, we think of the first idea of Elohim that saw the creation good, which is the idea of Ultimate Cause.

When we look at the ideas of God logically with contemporary knowledge of the universe, we find many differences from traditional ideas of God. We notice the earth has developed over billions of years. We notice the development of life on earth. We notice that life develops over generations. Each human generation develops more knowledge. Because of our mortality, we have morality to guide us to live together as long and well as we can.

Morality is our problem. We cannot avoid mortality. We work to make living as long and good as possible for everyone.

The idea of UC has been gradually developing and will continue to develop.

Ideas about God are attempts to know Ultimate Cause. Those seeking God are seeking Ultimate Cause of the universe.

We can mean UC when we say God. We can use the word God and not UC. That has been tried.

Only parts of the idea of UC have been used when this has been tried.

God is anything anyone wants the word "God" to mean. So you can mean Ultimate Cause when you say God. But no one will know unless you tell them. Ultimate Cause is not in human terms: a being, good, holy, perfect, infinite, moral, just, merciful, kind, gentle, all the time directly ordering and guiding events for his people. UC caused the earth to be as it is. Natural laws are reliable.

The word "God" is used to mean so many different things that we need to explain what we mean when we use it.

Ultimate Cause is capability to cause the universe to be as it is.

We know the universe from our experience and the information the sciences provide. UC likes and enjoys every thing about the universe.

It has been observed that believing in God is a bet on which you cannot lose. If God is like you believe, you win. If God does not exist, you have lost nothing.

However: It does make a difference what you believe and act upon about the universe, God, Ultimate Cause. People who believe God gives them land and instructs them to drive out the people who are there or kill them; People who believe God tells them to kill those who take their land; People who think those who do not believe in God as they do may be enslaved, imprisoned or killed; People who use force and threat of death to convert people and to keep them from changing their religion, cause a lot of grief. The people of the world loose a lot due to the people with such beliefs.

(Examples: inquisition, enslaving. killing those who are idolaters) (The Qur'an, Surah IX Repentance line 5, Numbers 31:15-19 The Princeton Seminary Bulletin Volume XXIV Number 2, New Series 2003 Page 231 on Columbus).

If you don't know UC, you lose experiencing the companionship of UC.

1. XENOPHANES

(480 BC) There is only one Ultimate Reality. The idea of God is not useful because there are many ideas of gods. Ultimate Reality would not have sense organs, but the whole of him would see, think, and hear. By the thoughts of the mind, Ultimate Reality would rule everything and be everywhere present. --- Internet: "Xenophanes", "The Internet Encyclopedia of Philosophy". http//www.iep.utm.eud/x.x-phanes.htm

2. A DICTIONARY OF THE BIBLE

by John D. Davis, published by The Westminster Press, copyright by the Trustees of the Presbyterian Board of Publications and Sabbath School Work, 1898-1920 says this about

God: 'This primary idea of God, in theism, is the product of that general revelation, which God makes of himself to all men, on the plane of nature. The truths involved in it are continually reiterated, enriched, and deepened in the Scriptures; but they are not so much revealed in them as presupposed at the foundation of the special revelation.'

This Dictionary passage also refers to "theistic proofs" which may refer to the Five Proofs of Thomas Aquinas, which really prove first cause. It refers to "sufficient cause for the contingent universe", of "an intelligent author of the order and of the manifold contrivances observable in nature," "on the principle of a sufficient cause."

This Dictionary passag indicate ideas that go back more than a hundred years and their use in religion. It gives the view that knowledge of nature is the foundation for knowing God (for theistic religions, for Christianity). It indicates that God is "sufficient cause of the universe";

"intelligent author of nature." It indicates the development of the idea of UC.

From: *The Westminster Dictionary of the Bible.* Used with permission from Westminster John Knox Press.

3. MARTIN LUTHER

Martin Luther describes a common point of view of God:

"When one asked; where God was before heaven was created? St. Augustine answered: He was in himself. When another asked me the same question, I said: He was building hell for such idle, presumptuous, fluttering and inquisitive spirits as you. After he had created all things, he was everywhere, and yet he was nowhere, for I cannot take hold of him without the Word. But he will be found there where he has engaged to be. The Jews found him at Jerusalem by the throne of grace, (Exodus xxv.) We find him in the Word and faith, in baptism and the sacraments; but in his majesty, he is nowhere to be found."
(Table Talk, # LXVII -- p. 28 A Compend of Luther's Theology by H.T. Kerr)

Notice the difference in Luther's idea of God and the idea of UC. UC is everywhere, observing everything. UC does not need to be found. We just need to be aware of UC's presence, as our companion.

In writing about God, "he was everywhere, and yet he was nowhere," Luther senses Ultimate Cause. Luther did not have the scientific knowledge of the universe we have, to think of God as abstract.

Another passage from Martin Luther:

"Many philosophers and men of great acumen have engaged in the endeavor to find out the nature of God; —all have gone blind over their task and failed of the proper insight. And, indeed, it is the greatest thing in heaven and on earth, to know God aright, if that may be granted to one.

How can one know God better than in the works in which He is most Himself? Whoever understands His works aright cannot fail to know His nature and will, His heart and mind."
("The Magnificat," Works of Martin Luther, Vol. III, p. 167 — Kerr p. 29)

We can see the longing in his writing. Did he see that God is most himself as cause of the universe? Apparently, Luther did not quite have it. No one is satisfied till he or she knows Ultimate Cause. We have knowledge of the universe that he did not have.

THE CHOICE

We have a choice: we can start with all the ideas of God and add the cause of the universe, Ultimate Cause or we think of Ultimate Cause directly.

God that is known by visions, dreams, revelations; is providential, hands on, chooses some people to be his people, commands, judges, sends to heaven or hell is different from -----Ultimate Cause of the whole universe that is known by inference from our knowledge of the universe: that caused the universe to be as it is; is objectively completely aware; likes and enjoys everything about the universe including every person unconditionally without judgment; is every persons' intimate companion experiencing with each person his/her every thought and feeling, preserving it all in memory beyond the existence of the universe; has the universe developing automatically by processes as a drama with people exploring, learning, developing astrophysics, stem cell therapies ---.

The greatest thought you or anyone will have is that Ultimate Cause of the whole universe is your companion. ("If that may be granted" you.)

From *A Compend of Luther's Theology*. Used with permission from Westminster John Knox Press.

4. JOHN CALVIN

John Calvin I.ii.2 (Kerr p5) writes:

"Cold and frivolous...are the speculations of those who employ themselves in disquisitions on the essence of God, when it would be more interesting to us to become acquainted with his character, and to know what is agreeable to his nature. For what end is answered by professing, with Epicurus, that there is a God, who, discarding all concern about the world, indulges himself in perpetual inactivity. What benefit arises from the knowledge of a God with whom we have no concerns? Our knowledge of God should rather tend first, to teach us fear and reverence; and secondly, to instruct us to implore all good at his hand and to render him the praise of all that we receive. For how can you entertain a thought of God without immediately reflecting, that, being a creature of his formation, you must, by right of creation, be subject to his authority? That you are indebted to him for your life, and that all your actions should be done with reference to him?"

From *A Compend of the Institutes of the Christian Religion by John Calvin*. Used with permission from Westminster John Knox Press.

Epicurus' idea of God fits UC in that to him the universe operates automatically. It would be interesting to know what more of his ideas fit UC, (See in *Modern Philosophy* p. 544 Hume's Inquiry and Associated Texts.)

John Calvin wanted an active, providential, miracle-working God. Ultimate Cause was not God such as John Calvin indicates he and other people wanted. He was right for his time for most people and until recently.

Now people who have knowledge of the universe from subatomic particles to galaxies of stars, from DNA to the many cultures of mankind, from geology to anthropology, who know that the universe is totally processes up to Ultimate Cause, are satisfied only in knowing Ultimate Cause. People who want to, can know UC is their most intimate companion experiencing with them their every thought and feeling, preserving the memory of their whole lives beyond the existence of the universe, While we accept our mortality we can think to and laugh to UC about the circumstances of our lives and think UC's response from our knowledge of the universe.

Ultimate Cause is not inactive but our companion, experiencing with us as we learn about the processes and learn to use them. We find we are responsible for learning about the natural laws and making the infrastructures that provide a good life for all people. We observe that the whole universe, including the earth and life of man, operates by natural laws. UC caused the natural laws we are trying to understand, formulate and use. We know things no one knew in Calvin's time. We know about electricity. We have sensors and recording devices that enable us to think of UC aware and remembering.

ACTIVE GOD

John Calvin points out that people have no use for an inactive God. People have ignored Ultimate Cause in favor of God that is providential, active in the affairs of man, works miracles, chooses people to be his people and favors his people over others. God has opposition. He is fighting evils that cause man's mortality. God enlists people to fight others who have different ideas of God.

Active God wants good for man but the earth and man have been corrupted by Satan. God wants, "The wolf will lie down with the lamb." God will make it so everything will be perfect for man to live forever without pain, suffering, or difficulties of any kind. God is actively working for his people when they ask. When people do not get what they ask for, they figure it is their fault or God will make it up to them in heaven. These ideas are the hope that comes with an active God.

Calvin and Luther did not have the view of the universe, the world and mankind developing by processes, as we do today.

5. THOMAS AQUINAS:

Thomas Aquinas gives five proofs of first cause (which is the same as Ultimate Cause). Then he wrote, "And this we call God." He had the start of the idea of Ultimate Cause.

6. JESUS:

Jesus presents heavenly Father as we think of Ultimate Cause, but did not go on to develop the idea of heavenly Father as Ultimate Cause. Jesus apparently foresaw the development of the idea of UC by the Holy Spirit, the comforter. There is no greater comfort than knowing UC is one's companion.

The hope to know God, is fulfilled in knowing Ultimate Cause of the whole universe. We know the capability of UC to have us in memory beyond the existence of this mortal universe.

If Mother Teresa had thought in terms of UC, she would not have thought of UC not existing.
If Martin Luther had thought in terms of UC, he would not have longed to know UC aright.
If John Calvin had known UC, he would not have thought of UC as an inactive God.
If Thomas Aquinas had not thought of first cause as God, he might have known UC.

APPENDIX 5
PROOF

DICTIONARY

The New Webster Encyclopedia Dictionary of the English Language (1952) page 666 gives the following definitions:

> *"proof,-- Any effort, process, or operation that ascertains truth or fact; a test; a trial; what serves as evidence; what proves or establishes; that which convinces the mind and produces belief ..."*

> *"prove,--- to establish the truth or reality of by reasoning, induction, or evidence;... to gain personal experience of; ... to attain certainty ..."*

The Britannica World Language Edition of *Funk and Wagnalls Standard Dictionary* (1958) gives these definitions:

> *"proof ---1--- the establishment of a fact by evidence or a truth by other truths.-- Evidence and argument sufficient to induce belief. . . ."*

> *"prove ---1 To show to be true or genuine, as by evidence or argument..."*

PROPERTIES OF PROOF

Proof is a process for ascertaining truth, reality, fact; presentation of evidence; giving of argument, reasoning; accepting evidence; accepting reasoning; results in convinced mind and belief; experiencing; certainty.

PROOF OF ULTIMATE CAUSE

THE EVIDENCE

The evidence is the universe from subatomic particles up to the greater universe of galaxies of stars. It is the earth with teaming cell life up to man with amazing cultures. It is the universe of matter, energy, time, space, gravity, magnetism, laws of nature, cause and effect, processes, creatures, man, mortality, and constant change.

We have found that man is rational. We have found that when we keep looking, we can find a cause for everything, up to the universe itself. We infer cause of the universe. We have found that everything in the universe is in process. We have found we can think objectively. We have found we can think of the abstract. We can think about Ultimate Cause.

REASONING

Our experience is that things do not cause themselves. The universe is a thing. The universe did not cause itself. The universe has cause that is neither the universe nor part of the universe. Phenomena have cause. The universe is phenomenon. The universe has cause. P has C, U = P, U has C.

Cause of the universe can be given the symbol C. Cause of the universe is not a phenomenon of the universe for which we can seek cause, therefore C is Ultimate Cause. (We cannot get outside the universe to observe what is there.) We infer properties of cause from properties of the phenomenon. We infer properties of C from our knowledge of the universe. C has properties that cause the universe. In our terms, C wanted, designed, made, is aware of everything, can intervene, likes, enjoys, remembers everything about the universe. These are the properties we would have if we were to cause the universe. We have no other way to think than in human terms.

ACCEPTANCE OF EVIDENCE

I accept the evidence. As evidence, I accept the universe as I experience it. I include in my experience the discoveries of the sciences. I accept the experiences of philosophers. I accept religious experiences. I include only things that make sense, that are rational. We are constantly acquiring new evidence. We need to encourage research of all kinds.

ACCEPTANCE OF REASONING

I accept the reasoning. Some people have said they reject Ultimate Cause because UC is a development of circular reasoning. Cause-and-effect reasoning is circular. More than that, it is back-and-forth. It is valid when there is a one-to-one relationship between the cause and effect, when either the cause or effect is observable, and the result is useful.

CONVINCED

I am convinced there is cause of the universe that we can designate Ultimate Cause, UC.

EXPERIENCE

I experience UC in my mind. I think of UC thinking with me and through me. I think UC experiences my pain, misery, and death with and through me. Thinking about UC gives me peace, amusement, and joy. UC is the center of my philosophy. Everything about the universe makes sense when I relate it to UC. The universe is a drama for UC to experience and enjoy. I am a part of that drama and am observing it with UC. The social and political structures of the United States of America are based on natural laws caused by UC. The result is the most dynamic and prosperous life on earth.

IMPENETRABLE CERTAINTY

I am convinced beyond a reasonable doubt. I have no doubt at all. UC is my companion. I think of UC experiencing with me the interesting things I see. UC experiences with me pain and misery. UC has me in memory beyond the existence of the universe.

SOME TESTS OF PROOF

Some tests of proof are: inclusive of all relevant information, consistency, and usefulness.

The idea of UC embraces all knowledge of the universe. It includes the whole universe and all people. It provides for growing knowledge of the universe by the sciences, experience, and reason.

The idea of UC is consistent. Every part points to Ultimate Cause. Knowing Ultimate Cause completes the quests of religion, science, and philosophy.

The concept of UC is useful. It promotes a common philosophy that leads to personal tranquility and social harmony. The United States of America, being based on Ultimate Cause, seeks to provide the best possible life for everyone.

PURE REASONING

Immanuel Kant, in his *'Prolegomena and Critique of Pure Reason'*, points out that pure reasoning proves nothing. The theses and antitheses are equally provable. The practical results of the use of the theses and antitheses show which is right.

The idea of Ultimate Cause meets the practicality test. Thinking in terms of UC brings personal tranquility and social harmony. The idea of UC as the basis of the United States of America's government and social structure provides the most prosperous and freest society the world has seen. The idea of Ultimate Cause is the base for the equality of man.

In section II: 'On the Ideal of the Highest Good, As a Determining Basis of the Ultimate Purpose of Pure Reason'. Kant writes about the third question:

"What may I hope?" "For all hoping aims at happiness. . . Hoping ultimately amounts to the conclusion that there is something (that determines the ultimate possible purpose) because something ought to occur; knowing ultimately amount to the conclusion that there is something (that acts as supreme cause) because something does occur."

One place this may be found is in: *Modern Philosophy: An Anthology of Primary Sources.* Edited by Roger Ariew and Eric Watkins, Hackett Publishing Company, Inc. Indianapolis/Cambridge 1998 p. 738, 741. (Used with permission).

Kant uses 'supreme cause' which we identify as Ultimate Cause. Kant uses 'ultimate possible purpose' which is the drama for Ultimate Cause. The ultimate purpose of pure reasoning, indeed of our being is for UC to enjoy experiencing each persons' unique life.

APPENDIX 6
JESUS CONTINUED
QUOTATIONS OF JESUS THAT FIT ULTIMATE CAUSE

1) ONE IN THOUGHT

"That they all may be one; as thou, Father, art in me, and I in thee, that they also may be one in us" (Jesus' prayer, John 17:21).

"Where I am there you may be also" (Jesus, John 14:3).

"—It is the spirit that quickens, the flesh profit nothing;" (Jesus, John 6:63).

"The kingdom of God is within you" (Jesus, Luke 17:21).

"As a man thinketh so is he" (Proverbs 23:7).

We are our thoughts. We are one with each other when we know each other, think alike, have the same ideas. We are one with UC as we have common thoughts. We have some of UC's thoughts, so UC is in us. UC has all of our thoughts, so we are in UC. We are in each other to the extent we have the same thoughts.

2) JUDGMENT

Jesus said, "—the Father judges no man,—" (John 5: 22)

Jesus said, "I judge no man." (John 8:15).

"Judge not, that ye be not judged." (Matthew 7:1).

"—ye shall know the truth and the truth shall make you free." (John 8:32).

"But I say to you, Love your enemies, bless them that curse you, do good to them that hate you, and pray for them which despitefully use you, and persecute you; that you may be the children of your Father which is in heaven: for he makes his sun to rise on the evil and on the good, and sends rain on the just and the unjust.--- Be ye therefore perfect, even as your Father in heaven is perfect." (Matthew 5:44–48).

Ultimate Cause does not judge. Jesus does not judge. We should not judge people. We are to love (enjoy) everyone. We are to work to make the social structures serve everyone. We want everyone to have the best possible life.

3) OMNIPOTENT

"—with God all things are possible." (Jesus, Matthew 19:26).
"—my Father is greater than I." (Jesus, John 14:28).
"I can of mine own self do nothing:" (Jesus, John 5:30).

UC caused the universe to be as it is, operating automatically by natural laws, but can intervene.

4) OMNIPRESENT

"---I am not alone, for the Father is with me." (Jesus, John 16:32).

Ultimate Cause is everywhere present in knowing all there is to know. UC knows our every thought and feeling. We do not need to seek UC. UC is our companion.

5) OMNISCIENT

"Heaven and earth shall pass away—But of that day and that hour knoweth no man, no, not, the angels which are in heaven, neither the son, but my Father only." (Jesus, Matthew 24:35-36; Mark 13:31-32).

"—sparrows – one of them shall not fall on the ground without your Father noticing. But even the hairs of your head are numbered." (Jesus, Matthew 10:29-30).

"—your Father knows what things you need before you ask him." (Matthew 6:8)

UC notices and is aware of everything. Ultimate Cause knows all there is to know. UC knows our every thought and feeling, is aware of every subatomic particle.

[It doesn't make sense to extend omniscience to God (heavenly Father, UC) to foreknow everything, so everything about the universe is following a script—is playing a record—nor that God, heavenly Father, UC guide every event of the universe and our lives. UC caused the universe to operate by natural laws. The universe is a drama for UC.]

6) ACCEPT OUR MORTALITY

"Father—not my will but thine be done." (Jesus' prayer, facing the cross. Luke 22:42)

"Do not think that I have come to bring peace on earth: I have not come to bring peace, but a sword." (Jesus, Matthew 10:34).

Everything we do and everything that happens to us is part of processes. UC caused the natural laws that make the processes. Whatever happens to us, including suffering and death, is for UC. We accept life for whatever it turns out to be. UC wants whatever happens. The processes of development go over generations. We do our part and pass it on to the next generation. UC experiences through us and with us every moment of our lives. The purpose of our being is for UC to experience each of our unique lives.

7) EARTHLY MORTALITY IS PAINFUL,

"My God, My God, why hast thou forsaken me?" (Jesus on the cross, Matthew 27:46).

"Father – I knew that you hear me always:" (Jesus, John 11:41-42).

"Father, into thy hands I commend my spirit:" (Luke 23:46).

"Father—not my will but thine be done." (Jesus, Luke 22:42).

We accept pain, suffering, and death as the will of UC. Jesus cried out in anguish. We do too. We know UC is always with us, experiencing everything with us.

Notice that Jesus said, God had forsaken him but heavenly Father was with him. The 'heavenly Father' idea is compatible with Ultimate Cause. God is hope. Ultimate Cause is logical certainty. If your idea of God is logically certain, that is the same as Ultimate Cause.

8) THOSE THAT HAVE THE MESSAGE OF GOD ARE GODS.

Jesus said, "If he called them gods, to whom the word of God came," (John 10:34-35). This refers to Psalm 82:1-4, 6-7:

"God is in the meeting-place of God; he is judging among the gods. How long will you go on judging falsely, having respect for the persons of evildoers? Give ear to the cause of the poor and the children without father; let those who are troubled and in need have their rights. Be the advisors of the poor and those who have nothing; take them out of the hand of the wicked. ---I said, you are gods; all of you are the sons of the Most High; But you will come to death like men, falling like one of the rulers of the earth."

The message connects the sender, messenger, and receiver. They become one in having the same message (thoughts). We become one with Jesus when we have the same ideas. We are one with UC to the extent that we have UC's view. (Actually, we are completely in UC. UC has all our thoughts and feelings.)

Here is the idea that gods are of the earth. People and judges are gods. Any authority or power may be termed god. Ultimate Cause is not of the earth and does not have children or sons. Such ideas are symbolic of the close relationship of thoughts shared by God, the gods. Ultimate Cause relates to people in shared thoughts.

Here also is the idea that judges, rulers are gods.

9) LOGOS

"In the beginning was the Logos (word), and the Logos was with God, and God was the Logos. This One was in the beginning with God. All things through Him came into being. – And the Logos flesh became and tabernacled among us," (John 1:1, 3, 14).

126

This is similar to the idea that C has something like thought put into something like words that brought all things into being. Things are the outcome of thought, Logos, word, command. Ultimate Cause caused the universe.

10) PEACE

"Peace I leave with you, my peace I give unto you; not as the world gives, give I unto you. Let not your hearts be troubled, neither let them be afraid." (Jesus, John 14:27).

We have peace of mind, tranquility, and harmony within ourselves and with others when we view as Ultimate Cause does. In some ways, Jesus had the view of Ultimate Cause. In some ways, he presents "our Father in heaven" as Ultimate Cause. In this, we have peace.

11) MORE TO COME

Jesus said, "I have yet many things to say to you, but you cannot bear them now. When the Spirit of truth comes, he will guide you into all truth." (John 16:12-13).

We now know some of the more that Jesus had to say. It is to know Ultimate Cause.

12) WE ARE UNITED IN WORK

"—whosoever shall do the will of my Father which is in heaven, the same is my brother, and sister, and mother." (Jesus, Matthew 12:50).

"Be not overcome of evil but overcome evil with good." (Paul in Romans 12:21).

"I am come that they might have life, and that they might have it more abundantly." (Jesus, John 10:10).

Jesus said, "Go ye therefor, and teach all nations,—" (Matthew 28:19).

Jesus in prayer said, "Father—this is life eternal, that they might know thee----." (John 17:1-3).

The idea of Ultimate Cause is for everyone. The Gospel, the Good News is that you have eternal life by knowing heavenly Father. This is true of UC. Since the universe is mortal, the only "never-ending" is Ultimate Cause beyond the existence of the universe.

You know you are in the memory of UC because you know UC is capable of knowing and remembering the whole life of every person, even our every thought and feeling. We are a drama for UC to enjoy. Our work is bringing about the time when everyone on earth has a full abundant life. It's coming, depends on knowing Ultimate Cause to which Jesus points in telling about the heavenly Father.

All the world's a stage. Our lives are a drama. The reason we exist is for Ultimate Cause to experience with each of us our unique lives. Ultimate Cause likes and enjoying each of us and preserves our whole lives in memory outside the universe. We know this when we know Ultimate Cause.

The plot of the play is mankind becoming self-aware, learning about the universe, making cultures that make life good for all people. The play is man developing. It is man discovering, learning, attaining skills, accumulating knowledge, using the resources of the earth to make life as good as possible for all people.

One really begins to enjoy living when one thinks in terms of Ultimate Cause. Jesus points to the Father in heaven that develops in our thoughts to Ultimate Cause.

APPENDIX 7
THESES AND FULFILLED HOPES

THESES

Based on rationality, cause and effect, processes, objectivity, abstract, natural laws, mortality and recycling, we know Ultimate Cause by inference from our knowledge of the universe. As our knowledge of the universe grows, so does our knowledge of UC. We know UC has capability to cause the universe to be as it is. We know UC in human terms. We have no other way. We think UC in causing the universe would have something like our experience making things. So UC would have thought of a universe, wanted a universe, have it designed, cause it to come into being, know all about it, like and enjoy it, remember everything about it.

UC is our companion, sharing our every thought, feeling, word, and deed. UC experiences with each of us all our joys and sorrows, pleasures and pains, failures and successes, defeats and victories. UC preserves our whole lives in constant awareness memory beyond the existence of the universe. This is the capability of UC. We think and talk to UC and think UC's response from our knowledge of the universe. The purpose of our being is for UC to experience with each person his or her unique life.

UC likes and enjoys everyone. UC does not judge. The universe is just as UC wants it. Ultimate Cause is not mortal so not moral. There is no evil to UC. Nothing hurts UC. We are part of the processes. We are mortal. In order to live as long and as well as we can, we are moral. Evil is very real to us and is our problem. Mankind developing from instinctive living to responsible self-conscious moral social living is the drama UC is enjoying. We can enjoy it too. Watching a baby develop into a responsible rational human being may be likened to UC watching the development of mankind from instinctive to rational responsible people.

FULFILLED HOPES

We have what thinking people through the ages have sought. We know what life is all about. We know cause of the universe. We know the universe is processes which operate by natural laws. We know cause of the universe is aware of every subatomic particle to human cultures. We know cause of the universe is our companion.

We are part of the drama of the universe. Ultimate Cause experiences with each of us our every thought, feeling, word and deed. The whole of our lives are preserved in UC's memory beyond the existence of the universe. This is not about ego; it is the capability of Ultimate Cause.

Mortality is the basis for morality. We are moral in order to live as long and as well as we can. We are individually and as communities responsible for morality. We hope to be providentially provided for but work on the basis of personal and social responsibility, based on natural laws.

JESUS

Jesus said he had more to say that the disciples could not understand. We now know some of that more. We know the universe is energy, subatomic particles, galaxies of stars, planets, plants, animals, people, cultures. "Cause of it all" likes and enjoys every part of it. We are to know, love, enjoy, and care for it.

Jesus, by example, shows us that we are to take part in the culture of our time and place. Jesus went to the temple and as a custom to the synagogue. Thinking in terms of God can be a stage in the development of knowing UC. Jesus knew "cause of all he knew of the earth" as the Father in heaven. Jesus said eternal life is to know the Father in heaven. In knowing Ultimate Cause, we know our whole lives are preserved in UC's memory beyond the existence of the universe. With UC, we enjoy the drama of the universe.

DAVID HUME

David Hume in, *An Inquiry Concerning Human Understanding*, 1789 wrote extensively about "cause". He points out that cause needs to be in exactly one to one relationship to the effect.

He also writes that he doubted that it is possible to know only from an effect (the universe) a cause (Ultimate Cause) so unique that no one has every known any other such a thing or cause.

(Modern Philosophy p..550)

We do what David Hume doubted could be done. We know Ultimate Cause.

LEWIS MUMFORD

Lewis Mumford wrote though most of the twentieth century. He was concerned about the future of the modern American, Western culture. He advocated extending democracy to everyone. He advocated orientating life beyond ambiguous moral conceptions to a higher meaning of life. He saw the need to make human life significant in the total cosmos. (Handbook p.283).

The things Mumford advocated are achieved in knowing Ultimate Cause. The ambiguous moral concepts are replaced by the natural laws of morality, based on our knowledge of human nature. Our lives can have no higher meaning than to know that we are important to Ultimate Cause. We are significant in the cosmos and beyond.

In our common companionship with UC we share companionship with everyone on earth and promote democracy.

JOHN CALVIN

John Calvin (1509-1564) *A Compend of the Institutes of the Christian Religion*, II.i.4: Kerr p. 42:

"We must consider the nature of Adam's sin... The prohibition of the tree of knowledge of good and evil was a test of obedience, that Adam might prove his willing submission to the divine government."

The warning to Adam not to eat of the tree of the knowledge of good and evil was that the idea of good and evil was dangerous. Man would misinterpret it. It would put man on the wrong path. Man would think in terms of God's law rather than rational morality based on mortality. Thinking in terms of God's law, good and evil, would make for conflict among people, rather than peaceful cooperation. People would be fighting each other in the name of God, over God's law. God would be choosing people to be his people. God would be blessing his people at the expense of others. God would be indicating his pleasure and displeasure by providential care or withholding providential care. Here also are the ideas of submission (slavery -- the slave mentality) and anti-knowledge.

Knowing Ultimate Cause corrects God given 'good and evil' that causes conflict among people.

Knowing UC changes slave mentality, submission, anti-knowledge to: freedom, development of knowledge, exploration of the world and universe, development of science and technology, education for everyone so everyone can prosper in democracy.

The heavenly Father and the teachings of Jesus do this. Jesus ended sacrifice by his own sacrifice. Jesus ended God laws with human laws sanctioned by the heavenly Father. See instructions described in Matthew 5;41-48 , and 'love your neighbor as yourself'.

JOHN CALVIN.

"Since God is first manifested, both in the structure of the world and in the general tenor of Scripture, simply as the Creator, and afterwards reveals himself in the person of Christ as Redeemer, hence arises a twofold knowledge of him; of which the former is first to be considered and the other will follow in its proper place." Kerr p. 5

We follow the first part of Calvin's idea in inferring UC from our knowledge of the universe. In my eighty years, I have noticed little mention about the structure of the world as the manifestation of God. Thinking in terms of UC, we know UC by inference from our knowledge of the universe.

From *A Compend of the Institutes of the Christian Religion* by John Calvin. Used with permission from Westminster John Knox Press.

THOMAS AQUINAS

Thomas Aquinas (1225-1274) was a Dominican monk born in Roccasecca, Italy, who studied in Naples, Cologne, and Paris. He wrote that "faith presupposes natural knowledge." Thomas Aquinas wrote five proofs of God. What he did was give five proofs of first cause from observations of nature. He then wrote, "this we call God."

The five proofs are that there is a first cause: (1) of change, (2) of causes, (3) of being, (4) that is a superlative of gradations, (5) that guides everything to observe natural laws. He concludes that this (first cause) everyone calls God.

Text of the five proofs can be found in: *Enduring Issues in Philosophy* by Gerald W. Eichhoefer (San Diego: Greenhaven Press, Inc., p. 139).

It is from St. Thomas Aquinas, *Summa Theologiae*, vol. 2, "Existence and Nature of God," question 2, articles 2, 3, translated by Timothy McDermott, O. P. London: Spottiswood, 1964. Copyright 1964 by the Blackfriars.

Thomas Aquinas, nearly 800 years ago, pointed out that St. Paul 1200 years previously had noted that truths about God can be known by our natural powers of reasoning and are presupposed to faith. He observed that "faith presupposes natural knowledge."

God has been considered creator for 3,000 years. Some people through the years thought of God as first cause. But I have found no one developed the idea of Ultimate Cause known by inference from our knowledge of the universe, till now. Here it is.

ENLIGHTENMENT

In knowing Ultimate Cause, you achieve the goal of enlightenment to be free and to know.

"Enlightenment—a term used to designate a period of great intellectual activity in the cause of general education and culture, including the preparatory self-emancipation from prejudice, convention and tradition." (Encyclopedia Britannica 1959, Vol. 8)

Knowing UC involves great intellectual activity, including general education and culture. It emancipates from prejudice, convention, and tradition.

ROMANTICISM

In knowing Ultimate Cause, you accomplish the goal of romanticism to achieve the height of elation and escape from unpleasant realities of mortality.

Romanticism: "In the late 18ᵗʰ century and 19ᵗʰ, a social and esthetic movement… that sought to free the individual from unpleasant realities by appealing to his aspirations for wonder and mystery. It emphasized a love for strange beauty, for the past and the far-away, and for the wild, irregular, or grotesque in nature, and found creative expression in spontaneity, lyricism, reverie, sentimentalism, mysticism and individualism."

(Funk and Wagnalls Standard Dictionary, Britannica World Language Dictionary, 1958)

In our companionship with UC, we think beyond the mortal universe. What is more wonderful and mysterious than cause of the universe? What is more personal than UC knowing our every thought and feeling? What is more irregular and far away and beyond nature than UC? What involves more of the past and future than UC? What could be more present and relevant than UC?

A Dictionary of the Bible by John D. Davis, Westminster Press 1920, gives this about God.

Used with permission from Westminster John Knox Press.

"This primary idea of God, in which is summed up what is known as theism, is the product of that general revelation, which God makes of himself to all men, on the plane of nature. The truths involved in it are continually reiterated, enriched, and deepened in the Scriptures; but they are not so much revealed in them as presupposed at the foundation of the special revelation –- On the plane of nature men can learn only what God necessarily is---."

Knowledge of nature (the universe) is presupposed at the foundation of the idea of God. The idea is that God would be inferred from knowledge of nature (the Universe). So God would be cause of the universe.

(The problem is that God is defined as more than can be inferred from knowledge of nature. So we need Ultimate Cause that we infer only by what we find in nature.)

THE WESTMINSTER CONFESSION OF FAITH

I grew up with *The Westminster Confession of Faith,* which starts out:

"Although the light of nature, and the works of creation and providence, do so far manifest the goodness, wisdom, and power of God, as to leave men inexcusable;---"

This indicates knowledge of nature, the universe (which includes providence, our having the necessities and good things in life) is sufficient to know God. So God would be cause of the universe.

(Again the problem is that God is defined as more than can be inferred from knowledge of nature. So we need Ultimate Cause that we know only by inference from our knowledge of the universe.)

I read some of the Westminster Confession of Faith at a youth meeting in my teens. Our pastor at the time when asked what he thought of it reacted, "It is boring." I new him well. He was interested in human relations. I think the problems of human relations will be solved by our common companionship with UC.

SCIENCE RELIGION CONFLICT

I remember talking with my father when I was about eleven. We were out along the lane leading to the pasture, inspecting and mending fence. I said to my father, "I have been hearing and reading that there is a religion/science conflict. It doesn't seem there could be. God created everything. Science is only trying to discover how things are. It doesn't make sense."

My father said, "It is true."

From that time, I have sought a way to reconcile science and religion. The solution is to know Ultimate Cause. When we have UC's point of view, everything has its place.

UC likes and enjoys all the religions and the sciences. UC enjoys the drama of our coordinating all our ideas logically so we live rationally. When we live rationally, governments operate according to natural laws, the way people are. The sciences objectively research and experiment to describe every aspect of the universe, including man. Religions develop cultures that include knowing the universe as the sciences find it, inferring Ultimate Cause from that knowledge.

Ultimate Cause made us so we develop both religion and science. Accept them both. Each contributes to our lives. When everyone knows UC and has UC's view, everything makes sense. We all work together to have a rational world culture that provides for everyone an opportunity to participate and have the most comfortable life possible. Religions and the sciences are free to function.

THE SOUL

When I was about thirteen, I heard several speakers at church talk about the soul. I wondered what they meant. They seemed so certain they knew what they were talking about. Everyone seemed satisfied.

Through the years, I have noted the use of the word. I have wondered what they meant. The dictionary indicates the word *soul* is used in various ways. Soul may mean: the spirit and immortal part of man; the moral and emotional part of man; the seat of sentiment or feeling. The soul may include conscience, will, desires, longings, fears, loves, hopes, animation, spirit, courage, sense of honor. The soul may be the activity of DNA that starts at conception and ends when it ceases.

The soul may be the breath of life, existing when breath begins and ending when breath stops. The soul may be awareness, mental functioning, reasoning, the mind. The soul may be rationality, starting when one understands and ends when one ceases to understand. The soul has been defined as beginning when one has faith, is born again.

My conclusion is that the soul is the mind: all the thoughts one has, the furniture of the mind, one's virtual reality.

UC has every person's total mind (with all the changes of his or her whole life) (soul) in memory beyond the existence of the universe. Ultimate Cause is complete soul, total soul. UC has the whole universe in mind. UC has every person's whole life of thoughts and feelings (virtual reality) in memory beyond the existence of the universe.

APPENDIX 8
PHILOSOPHERS

These philosophers are cited to provide a glimpse into the history of the development of thinking skills and the idea of UC.

From *Handbook in the History of Philosophy 3500 BC to the Present* by Albert E. Avey, Second Edition, 1961 Barnes & Noble, Inc.

The earliest records we know of about what we technically call philosophical thought in the Western world was by the Greeks about 600 BC. They thought abstractly and with exactness, made reflective analysis and started what we call the sciences and mathematics.

1) p. 8 Zoroaster (660-583 BC) saw in all the processes of the universe a continual struggle between good and evil, truth and falsehood. The Hebrews may have from this during the exile developed the idea of Satan as the great adversary of Jehovah. [processes]

2) p. 10 Thales (624-550 BC) sought to know Ultimate Reality, the basic stuff of which things are made, which he concluded by his observation is water. None of his writings remain. Aristotle held that he made his conclusion on the basis of his observation that there is so much water, its power and importance for life. The important thing about Thales is that he did his own thinking. He relied on his own observations and reasoning. He did not appeal to tradition, religion, or poetry. He is thought to be the first *hylozoist (idea that all matter is alive)*. [Each person knows for him- or herself.] [Thales did not, as far as we know, think of what we call subatomic particles. But they do make matter alive (active).]

3). p. 12 Pythagoras (500 BC) had idea of solar system.

4) p. 13 Xenophanes (570-480 BC) decided there is only one Ultimate Reality. He noticed the different ideas of gods. They could not be the true concept of God. He must be one and not like any particular finite being, man or animal. God must not have sense organs like men's, but "the whole of him sees, the whole of him thinks, the whole of him hears." He rules all things by the power of his mind; and he is

omnipresent, not needing organs of locomotion. He suggested a theory of evolution having observed fossils on a mountainside. [Had much of the idea of UC, things develop.]

5) p. 13 Heraclitus (500 BC) saw that everything is changing in an orderly way regulated by rational Logos. [Rationality, reason, objectivity, harmony, had much of the idea of UC.]

6) p. 14 Parmenides (about 495 BC) taught that ideas are the same as being, which is the basis of idealism. [Thought is reality, idealism. Non-mortal is real, so is thought, Virtual Reality.]

7) p. 15 Anaxagoras (425 BC) taught that the order in nature is due to an ordering mind (Nous). In nature, he saw biological evolution. [Here is the idea of design, mind, evolution, omnipresence.]

8) p. 17 Leucippus (approx. 449 BC) saw in nature reason and cause. [Cause and necessity, cause and effect.]

9) p. 21 Socrates (400 BC) "The unexamined life is not to be lived." Questioned in order to have definite meaning. Words have to be defined in order to know what is being talked about. [Induction, universal principles.]

10) p. 23 Aristippus (approx. 395 BC) taught that feelings and pleasures are the best part of life. [Experience.]

11) p. 25 Plato (427-347 BC). His real name was Aristocles. Taught that ideas are eternal. [Ideas are eternal, analysis, abstract, rationality, ultimate one, moving picture, universe a stage.]

12) p. 29 Eudoxus (408-355 BC) calculated the length of the year as 365 days and 6 hours. Saw the planets moved in concentric circles. [Planetary system.]

13) p. 31 Aristotle (384-322 BC) formulated the idea of the syllogism, the combination of two premises in order to draw a conclusion. He developed deduction and demonstrated the process of induction. He developed the idea of the logic of science which aims at truth as a field for application of the syllogism. He wrote about dialectic which deals with probable premises. He dealt with the problems of continuous process,

numbers as infinite in terms of possible addition, space as infinitely divisible. He dealt with motion and change by a first mover which is itself unmoved. The process of change which occurs constantly in the physical world indicates there are no absolute origins and cessations, only a transition of substance from one form to another. In his writing, he concluded that God is ultimately thought, completely self-conscious, eternal, one, the highest form, and pure actuality. He concluded that eudaemonia or happiness consists of contemplative leisure. [Syllogism, induction, processes, first mover, ultimate thought, happiness.]

14) p. 41 Zeno of Citium (335-265 BC) established the school in the Stoa Poikile (Painted Porch) at Athens; whence the name "stoic." He held that human reason is identical in essence with a world reason that pervades the universe and keeps it in order. This is the Divine Reason, or the Logos (word). The material real world is pervaded by force. All things are animated by a universal soul. He wrote about the causal law of the universe... Man's obligation is to live rationally and accept nature as an orderly expression of world reason or providence, submitting without complaint to what it brings. [Human reason same as world reason, as divine reason, as Logos, universal soul, cause of the universe, rationality, don't complain about what happens, providence.]

15) p. 42 Strato (A. 288-268 BC) insisted that nature itself is God.

16) p. 44 Aristobulus (181-146 BC) regarded God as invisible and transcendent. [Transcendent, outside, beyond the universe.]

17) p. 45 Titus Lucretius Carus (95-55 BC) wrote that at death, the body dissolves and all is at an end; there is no hereafter to be feared.

18) p. 53 Epictetus (60-117 AD) taught the recognition of the course of nature as the will of God, recommended the acceptance of that which is not within man's power—held that the human will is the one thing under man's control, whereby he can determine the attitude he takes towards the vicissitudes of life. Man should view all men as if they had similar capacities and similar problems and, therefore, as if they were essentially equal. As a slave, he is reported to have said to his master who was twisting his leg, "If you keep twisting, it will break." [Objectivity, accept what comes, equality of people.]

19) p. 54 Flavius Justinus (105-165) held that a rational power, the Logos, is produced by God and disseminated through all men. They have thereby an innate consciousness of God. All men who live according to this Logos are Christians, regardless of where or when they live, even though they be called atheists. [Logos is universal is rational power.]

20) p. 55 Marcus Aurelius (121-180) wrote that to maintain peace of mind, believe in a rational world order directed by providence, and be unafraid of death, which is a natural occurrence. And resign oneself to the will of God and love all mankind. [Rationality, providence, processes. Love, enjoy.]

21) p. 58 Tertullian (c. 160-230) used the thought "It is certain because it is impossible." He therein put faith above reason. [Faith above reason.]

22) p. 61 Plotinus (205-270) held that God is the Ultimate Reality, a spirit so lofty that He is beyond all finite description. The nearest approach is to speak of Him as One, the Infinite Cause from which all finite things emanate. [Ultimate Reality, Infinite Cause.]

23) p. 68 Aurelius Augustinus (354-430). St. Augustine held that God transcends human comprehension. The universe is not an emanation from God, but a creation out of nothing. All things were created instantaneously, but not in their full reality. Only in time are the potentialities fully actualized. Time itself was created; there was no time before creation. Evil has its place in the structure of things, and therefore contributes to the final goodness of the universe. [Universe created out of nothing, development, processes, time created, evil part of the universe.]

24) p. 72 Dionysius (6th century) reckoned time according to the Christian era.

25) p. 74 Gregory the Great (540-604) made the papacy a temporal power, revised church music. He clarified the doctrines of angelology, purgatory, the Eucharist, and relics.

26) p. 76 Mohammed (570-632), dissatisfied with the moral condition of the people around him, preached a new doctrine—of one absolute God, Ruler, and Judge of the world. He denounced idolatry and infanticide. He added military power to his preaching and extended his power to surrounding countries. His chief doctrines expounded belief in Allah, angels, the prophets of Allah, the Koran, divine decrees, and a final judgment. The duties of the followers are: repetition of the simple creed, prayer five times a day, almsgiving to other Moslems, fasting, and a pilgrimage to Mecca. The Koran advocates abstention from wine, music, and pork, and commends labor and poverty. [One God, Ruler, Judge.]

27) p. 77 Severus Sebokht (A. 650) [Mesopotamia] made the first reference to Hindu numerals. Apparently the symbol for zero was not known to him.

28) p. 77 Bede the Venerable (672-735) [Jarrow] determined the date of Easter.

29) p. 84 Anselm (1033-1109) argued that 'the Being than whom no greater can be though' must exist, by definition, for an unrealized idea is not as great as a realized one. This is called the ontological argument for the existence of God. This was criticized by Kant and others saying a definition logically, has no existential import. Anselm held that revelation lays a basis for reason and that one must accept the beliefs of the church before one can undertake to understand them. This puts orthodoxy prior to inquiry. All articles of faith, once adopted, can be proven by logic alone. [Pure logic can prove anything, pro or con — Kant.]

30) p. 85 Manegold of Lautenbach (A. 1084 – c. 1103) opposed the use of dialectic, and held that theology is not subject to logic. Logic can not produce certitude on any question; certitude rests on revelation as found in the scriptures. He held most philosophy is superfluous. [Part of this is confirmed by Kant in that pure reason can prove and disprove theses and antitheses alike; experience makes the difference.]

31) p. 87 Peter Abelard (1079-1142) had the idea that God created everything from an inner necessity of his own being. He held that the moral quality of an act lies not in the act itself, but in its intention. [Creation comes from inner necessity of creator.]

32) p. 91 Averroes (ibn Ruschd) (1126-1198) [Cordoba, Seville, Morocco] regarded religion as an allegorical world view for common man, beyond which the philosopher seeks the deeper truth.

33) p. 93 Amalric of Bena (d. 1204) [Chartres, Paris] held that every man as well as Christ is an apparition of God, a member of Christ. [All one in thought.]

34) p. 94 William of Auvergne (A. 1220-1249) [Aurillac, Paris] opposed the Arabic doctrine of the eternity of the world. [Cause of universe.]

35) p. 94 Alexander of Hales (c. 1180-1245) had the idea that God is pure activity without matter and form. [C not part of universe.]

36) p. 97 John of Fidanza (St. Bonaventure) (1221-1274) [Bagnora, Paris] held that we rise from the knowledge of creatures to a knowledge of God the Cause and Creator of nature. [Cause, creator.]

37) p. 98 Thomas Aquinas (1225-1274) [Roccasecca, Cologne, Paris, Rome] had essentially two points in his theory of knowledge. One was facts of nature, which reason is competent to deal with. The second is that which deals with truth beyond nature, and which must be revealed to faith, e.g., the mysteries of the Christian doctrine. These two are not opposed to each other, but faith must set in where reason reaches its limit. According to the writings of Thomas Aquinas, the process of reasoning is fundamentally inductive, beginning with the data presented by sense and passing to ever larger generalizations into science and philosophy. Science is knowledge of facts by way of general principles. Philosophy is knowledge of ultimate things by way of reason. Theology has two divisions: (1) natural, which can be understood by reason, and (2) revealed, which must come through faith which reaches beyond reason. Universals exist before things in the mind of God. The world was created out of nothing, as were space and time. The existence of God can be proved by way of the concepts of an Original Mover, a First Cause, a Necessary Being, and a Higher Perfection.

The highest good is the happiness which comes from the knowledge and the love of God. An acceptable form of state is one that includes the education of the citizens and the maintenance of freedom from economic want.

38) p. 104 Dietrich (Theodoric) of Freiberg (c. 1250?) formulated the theory that the rainbow is formed by the diffraction and reflection of sunlight by raindrops. [Spectrum.]

39) p. 108 William Ockham (1280-1349) Knowledge of individual things must be intuitive, and in understanding things one must not employ a plurality of concepts beyond necessity. This is know as "Ockham's Razor."

40) p. 114 Leonardo da Vinci (1452-1519)[Vinci, Florence] enunciated basic principles such as heliocentric astronomy. He held that mathematical investigation and technique must replace traditional speculation... Experience and experiment are the basis of science. Certainty comes only with mathematical formulation, and the culmination of mathematics is mechanics, drawing conclusions from cause to effect and vice versa. [Cause and effect.]

41) p. 115 Desiderius Erasmus (1466-1536) [Rotterdam, Paris, London, Basel] advocated return to a simple Christianity, free from ecclesiastical ceremonial. He was the embodiment of faith in liberal studies and freedom of thought.

42) p. 117 Martin Luther (1483-1546) [Eisleben, Wittenberg, Worms] was convinced that salvation is through faith alone. [Ideas save.]

43) p. 119 John Calvin (1509-1564) stood for the absolute sovereignty of God, (in history and in life, and for the complete dependence of man upon God's will. Man has freedom to yield to this will, but the conditions of his salvation are determined by God). Salvation comes through the working of the grace of God. [Complete sovereignty of God.]

44) p. 121 Jacob Zabarella (1532-1589) [Padua] believed in an original matter infinite in extent and eternal in existence. Knowledge has two levels, natural objects and elaborations which result from reflection. It

is with the latter that logic deals; the sciences are applied logic working in two directions between cause and effect. [Cause and effect.]

45) p. 122 Francisco Patrizzi (Patricius) (1529-1597) [Dalmatia, Padua, Ferrara, Rome] hoped by his philosophy to reconcile science and Christian faith. [Reconciliation of science and religion.]

46) p. 125 Jacob Boehme (1572-1621) [Altseidenberg] saw the world as a manifestation of God who is both transcendent and eminent. He believed that heaven and hell are on earth. He who renounces evil and develops from darkness to light, is already in heaven; he who clings to evil is already in hell. [Ultimate Cause is present but not part of the universe.]

47) p. 128 Galileo Galilei (1564-1642) formulated the law of the Isochronism of a pendulum, wrote on the center of gravity of solids, and established fundamental laws of dynamics. With his telescope, he showed the mountains on the moon, discovered the satellites of Jupiter, and concluded that the Milky Way is composed of stars. He observed the form of Saturn, the phases of Venus, and the spots on the sun. His discoveries led to questions regarding consistency with scriptures. He defined the meaning of cause and effect. [Cause and effect.]

48) p. 133 Pierre Gassendi (1592-1655). Atoms were created by God out of nothing and were given an indestructible impulse toward movement,. The order of nature comes from God. Science is concerned with secondary causes. [Created out of nothing, science deals with secondary causes.]

49) p. 133 Thomas Hobbes (1588-1679) developed a theory of the state. It begins with the assumption that men are by nature self-seeking and hostile toward each other. Yet finding constant hostility intolerable, they form a contract and turn over the enforcement of it to a sovereign power, to which men are thereafter irrevocably bound to be loyal in all circumstances.

50) p. 134 James Harrington (1611-1677) selected property, especially in land, as the basic determiner of power.

51) p. 134 Blaise Pascal (1623-1662) wrote that sense and reason deceive each other. Then feeling functions, bringing satisfaction. Religious feeling is independent of understanding. In it alone is there peace. Pascal asserted that the belief in God is a wager on which one can lose nothing.

52) p. 135 Joseph Glanvil (1636-1680) held that the attempt to grasp the whole system of things through reference to their causes is necessarily impossible. All facts are isolated without necessary connection with any other.

53) p. 136 John Sergeant (1622-1707) defended the immediate knowledge of things through pure understanding and reason.

54) p.138 Baruch Spinoza (1632-1677) concluded the State can by force determine overt action, but it cannot by the same means compel one to think certain thoughts; democracy is the form of government that is most true to humanity... He concluded that "substance," the ultimate subject of discourse, is infinite, and there cannot be more than one. This substance is God, or nature, and has an infinite number of attributes; to us, the most important are extension and thought.. The Ultimate Substance is neither matter nor mind. He reasoned that man is so closely caught up in the structure of the universe that his only real freedom is intellectual, the freedom to contemplate and understand. Reason is the distinguishing mark of the human animal; the highest good of life, the goal of ethics, is to live according to reason and to perfect so far as possible the development of reason. Emotion is the disturbing factor in life, and what emotions need more than anything else is rational control. Emotions lead men to live by the impulse of the moment instead of eternity. Domination of man by the emotions alone is "human bondage"; rational ordering of the emotions is human freedom. To achieve this is difficult, "But all things excellent are as difficult as they are rare."

The highest form of religion is the rational contemplation of God, or understanding nature; He expressed worship not by way of emotion, but by way of intellect. For man as a rational creature, the most appropriate love of God is intellectual.

55) p. 141 Sir Isaac Newton (1642-1727) contributed to the development of calculus and the spectrum. He put together the theory of universal gravitation and the laws of motion and developed the telescope. He believed the existence of God is indicated by the order of the universe, as in the solar system and in the organs and behavior of animals. [Spectrum.]

56) p. 147, George Berkeley (1685-1753) said we assume there is an Omnipresent Mind observing the universe. He conceded that knowledge of spirit is not attainable by way of idea, but by way of a reflective process, which he designates by the term "notion" instead of "idea." Idea signifies the passive object of sense knowledge, whereas notion indicates the active side of the knowing process. [Omnipresent mind.]

57) p. 149, G.W. Leibniz (1664-1716) believed the universe is the expression of Perfect Reason. Therefore, it must be the best of all possible worlds. All apparent evil would be transformed by a larger view of the universe. [No ultimate evil.]

58) p. 152, Matthew Tindal (c. 1656-1733). His treatise has been called the "bible" of deism; Tindal expounded the doctrine of "natural religion" (religion of reason), consisting of ideas based on rational knowledge without appeal to revelation and opposing subjective belief. He observed that natural religion is implicated in the constitution of the world and the nature of God and man; hence, it is intrinsic and not dependent upon historical occurrences. Reason is a natural light by which God is necessarily known. Tindal believed this to be presupposed by revealed religion itself. [Reason, rational.]

59) p. 153 John Gay (1669-1745) wrote that the moral sense which men have is not innate but is acquired from experience, their own or others'.

60) p. 153 David Hume (1711-1776) said proof can never be adequate. He contended that the so-called dictate of natural law in morals is only the dictate of social utility.

61) p. 158 Francis Hutcheson (1694-1747) was the first to use the phrase "the greatest good for the greatest number."

62) p. 158 Edmund Burke (1729-1797) maintained that members of parliament are not instruments of their constituents, but men chosen by them to think independently for the good of the Commonwealth.

63) p. 160 Adam Smith (1723-1790) rests moral judgment on sympathy, the ability of a spectator to participate in the feelings of the actor, and to accept the end of the action.

64) p. 161 Jean Jacques Rousseau (1712-1778) maintained that the state came into existence through an agreement among men upon conditions of living together. In the condition of nature, all men are equal, but through the influence of society and civilization, they become unequal. [All equal before UC.]

65) p. 162 Thomas Reid (1710-1796). All knowledge is built upon principles that are self-evident and every man with common sense is aware of such principles. Reid recognized causality as one such principle, and belied it should be subjected to criticism. [Causality.]

66) p. 163 Moses Mendelssohn (1729-1786) [Dessau, Berlin] was a pioneering advocate in Germany on behalf of the emancipation of the Jews, the separation of church and state.

67) p. 164 Lord Monboddo (1714-1799) [Edinburgh] said man is of the same species as the orangutan, but man has gradually advanced from the animal condition, in which mind is immersed in matter, to a level on which mind acts independently of the body, and to a social state determined by the needs of human life. In addition, he noted that language is a product of social living. [Mind is independent of the body.]

68) p. 165 Immanuel Kant (1724-1804) in astronomy formulated a nebular hypothesis to account for the evolution of the physical universe. Kant saw that Hume had tried to reduce to phenomena (or sensory appearances), what can never be so reduced, namely the presuppositions or prior frameworks which determine for phenomena the form they have. There can be no specific items in space and time for one who has no capacity to perceive space and time. The assertion "this is an instance of spatiality" is impossible without the assumption of a logically prior general idea of spatiality. Kant says: no doubt all

knowledge begins with experience, but it does not follow that all comes from experience. Certainly our belief in the infinity of space and time is not a belief that has been empirically verified. The capacity to have experiences of a spatial and temporal character is an *a priori* possession of the knower. The particular occasions for exercising these capacities and the particular contents which result are *a posteriori* factors in experience. Knowledge is the result of interplay of the two.

As in the case of perception, the kind of experience one gets is determined primarily by the structure of perceiving, so in the intellectual processes the fundamental thing is the kind of structure knowledge-activity exhibits. Since the forms of perception and thought are due to the structure of the knower, it follows that they can give no knowledge of things-in-themselves (noumena) beyond experience.

Morality consists of actions in accordance with principles. An unprincipled man is an immoral man. And principle here as in science is the principle of consistency, necessity, and universality. "So act that the maxim of thy deed may stand as universal law."

Respect as ultimate the humanity of every man. Never regard humanity as a means to something else, but always as the final end.

Morality is concerned with what ought to be, not with what is; it cannot be derived from description of human behavior. It is prescriptive, not descriptive. The moral value of a life cannot be measured by its everyday success; it must be measured by its degree of embodiment of principle. A life lived according to principle is good, regardless of material success or failure. Ultimately, the only good thing in the world is a good will. Duty is the key word, not pleasure, and the imperative call of duty is categorical, not conditional. Morality presupposes certain postulates of practical reason. Above all, freedom is assumed.

Second, immortality is presupposed because it is impossible to meet the demand "be perfect" in any finite life. If the moral law makes an impossible demand, then it is irrational and cannot be moral. Thirdly, since this life shows much injustice to those who are most deserving, there must be belief in a God who will finally see that justice is done or there will be a eternal rift in the moral structure of the universe.

[Instead of judgment and justice, the universe is a drama for UC.]

In his *Modern Philosophy, an Anthology of Primary Sources,* edited by Roger Ariew and Eric Watkins, (Hackett Publishing, 1998) "Critique of Pure Reason," Kant indicates he takes for granted that God is Ultimate Cause. He uses the words, "supreme intelligence" (p. 739), "supreme cause" (p. 741), "supreme reason" (p. 743), "supreme cause" (p. 744), "supreme will" and "omnipotent, omniscient, omnipresent" (p. 744) "concept of a single original being", "independent cause or of a wise ruler of the world" (p. 745), "wise originator of the world" (p. 747). (We remember that many of the philosophers wrote not in English but are translated.)

69) p. 171 Jeremy Bentham (1748-1832) held that the interests of the individual are inseparable from those of the community. The act, the circumstances, the intention, and the consciousness must be taken into account in estimating the moral value of an action. All virtue is based on prudence and benevolence. Bentham's ethics was based upon regard for consequences, whereas Kant's was based upon principle.

70) p. 172 John Fichte (1762-1814) held that man walks by faith not by sight; they live by what they believe, rather than by what they know. The moral interests of man must take precedence over his scientific interests. The world of appearances in space and time is posited by Absolute Spirit as the objectification of its will. What is beyond us is Absolute Mind. In society, these various finite selves come into conflict with each other. Consequently, it is the function of morality and law to regulate these conflicts. In addition, he stated that it is the function of intelligence to educate citizens so that they see the necessity for the limitations that are placed upon them. The intelligent citizen freely and willingly accepts the restraints of law and considers them as self-limitations, not external obstacles to action.

71) p. 178 Johann Friedrich Herbart (1776-1841) held the Real to be irreducible units of being. The universe is pluralistic, not monistic. He considered a soul one of the Reals and he credited it with expressing its own self-preservation through its ideas. Freedom is the dominance of the strongest mass of idea.

72) p. 179 W. F. Hegel (1770-1831) considered reality as living, evolving process. The Absolute is Universal Reason moving through eternity and embodying itself in the actual universe, thought and being are one. That the universe is rational, as indicated by the order seen in the heavens, in the laws of biology, in all things; and it is the function of philosophy to comprehend the reason in these things. Thinking is essentially an inductive process. Spirit reaches its absolute stage and its highest self-realization in art, religion, and philosophy. Art renders the infinite visible, religion symbolizes it as more than art, and philosophy brings it under the mastery of thought. [Rational.]

73) p. 182 Albert Schopenhauer (1788-1860) read Buddhist works and related that they were truthful when they said that life is a process of desire and—in the nature of the case—could never be satisfied. Life in its essence is movement and restlessness. Therefore, a fair-minded man will necessarily be pessimistic because of the hopelessness of ever finding satisfaction in life. There is no ultimate escape from pessimism, but there are three approximate means. Art which includes music, which is especially valuable, for it combines most completely the eternity of art and the restless movement of life. But the evil of life maintains itself in the fact that one cannot live at every moment on a high level of artistic appreciation. Sympathy is a second escape from pessimism. It subordinates selfish individualism and minimizes the conflicts of living. It effects in some degree a unity among men, and constitutes a basis for ethics. A third is to renounce the very will to live. Not suicide, but an attitude of complete indifference to living.

74) p. 188 Bernard Bolzano (1781-1884) opposed a subjective interpretation of truth and supported the conception of truth-in-itself, existing independently regardless of whether it is known or not. He believed that even the omniscient mind of God acknowledges this. [UC's mind, memory, thought of, planned U.]

75) p. 191 John Stuart Mill (1806-1873) [London, Avignon] regarded the first principles of mathematics as hypothetical rather than certain. The law of causation is nothing but invariable sequence. The syllogism of traditional logic is a bit of circular reasoning because the major premise would have to be established by induction, which would include the conclusion in its summary. Caution is needed in saying one

or the other even is cause; both may be effects of a common cause. He expected the ethical goal to be the greatest happiness for the greatest number.

76) p. 195 Jacob Moleschott (1822-1893) [Zurich] held that physical conditions are the chief determinants in human life. Matter conditions life, life conditions thought, and thought conditions the will to improve.

77) p. 196 George Boole (1815-1864) reduced logic to a kind of mathematics with two quantities, 1 and 0. 1 represents the universe of thinkable objects. Propositions were reduced to equations, and precise deductions were made in accordance with rule, in a system analogous to algebra, and developed a theory of probability.

78) p. 201 Herbert Spencer (1820-1903) [London]. In society, the whole serves the individual parts, whereas in the individual organism, the parts serve the whole. Perfect life is marked by a maximum variety of interests and the longest possible duration.

79) p. 205 Karl Marx (1818-1883) [Treves, Paris, Brussels, London] presented an interpretation of the historical trend in social structures. The social and economic situation contemporary with his early life was capitalism, which had been furthered by the Industrial Revolution. He believed capitalism to be only a temporary phase which would pass away into socialism, when the proletariat (workers) became intolerant of their exploitation by the heads of industry. He thought that the working classes around the world should become conscious of their common interests and develop an international solidarity that would oppose traditional idealism by substituting an ideology which centers in economic determinism and by recognizing the struggle between economic classes. This struggle is a concrete, practical dialectic and will go on until it develops a classless society—in which a man is no longer a commodity, in which the wholeness of each human life may be realized. (*Das Kapital,* 1867)

"Dialectical materialism: A socio-economic theory introduced by Karl Marx and Friedrich Engels, according to which history and the forms of society are interpreted as the result of conflicts between social classes arising from their relations to the means of production." *Britannica World Language Dictionary*, 1958

80) p. 205 Noah Porter (1811-1892) had the idea that the universe is a thought as well as a thing and maintained that everyone must assume the existence of God in order that thought and science may be possible. (To me, this indicates that God is something like thought or UC.)

81) p. 210 Paul Janet (1823-1899) recognized the validity of final causes in life and mind.

82) p. 215 Chauncey Wright (1830-1875). Scientific ethics should be free from fears and aspirations and, at the same time, be purely objective. [Objectivity.]

83) p. 217 Arthur J. Balfour (1884-1930) [Cambridge, London] maintained that science rests on postulates accepted on faith, as religion does. Both are based on "inevitable beliefs." Science, like religion, postulates a rational Ultimate Cause of the World. In 1915, he published *Theism and Humanism*. [Ultimate Cause postulated by Science and Religion – Religion by faith and Science by logic.]

84) p. 221 James Martineau (1805-1900) [Liverpool, London]. His view was that causality is not merely phenomenal; it is grounded in a non-phenomenal world. [UC not phenomena.]

85) p. 221 Francis Ellingwood Abbot (1836-1903) [Boston] was one of the founders of the Free Religion Association, which was devoted: (1) to the study of rational religion without priests, (2) to a moral code independent of theology, (3) to a god without dogmatic systems, and (4) to a religion of action. [I suggest a religion for fellowship and independent study of idea.]

86) p. 228 Francis H. Bradley (1846-1924) [Oxford] held that the Whole is in every experience. The Absolute is super-personal, containing all history and progress, though not subject to these. [This suggests to me the idea of UC aware of everything, and in memory remembers everything.]

87) p. 230 Wilhelm Ostwald (1853- 1932) [Leipzig]. The properties of matter are special manifestations of energy (chemical, electrical, etc.). He described consciousness as another manifestation. Interaction between the physical and mental is possible as transition from one form of energy to another.

88) p. 236 David Hilbert (1862-1943) said that mathematics is a process of manipulation of symbols, without content, in accordance with certain rules. Simply, it is a kind of game played with marks on paper.

89) p. 240 Max Planck (1858-1947) introduced to science the concept of "quantum"—the unit in which energy travels—which is comparable to an atom of matter. He formulated the following: the magnitude of the quantum of radiant energy of a given frequency is equal to the product of the frequency multiplied by his constant h.

90) p. 240 Edmund Husserl (1859-1938) [Gottingen]. To Husserl, analysis of consciousness reveals that it involves an act of being conscious, an object of consciousness, and a datum by which the object is known. The object is given, not constructed by consciousness, and is not the "appearance" of any "reality." It is the content of "pure" experience.

91) p. 241 Josiah Royce (1855-1916) [California, Cambridge]. The primary problem of philosophy is the problem of knowledge. Knowledge is more than perception and conception; it is interpretation. The movement from the general and incomplete "internal meaning" of an idea to the concrete and perfected "external meaning" is the attainment of the Real, which is the goal of the idea. This Royce named as the aim of every philosophical system, although different temperaments follow different paths in order to reach it. Fundamentally, the temperaments are four: the realistic, the mystical, the critical rationalistic, and the synthetic idealistic. Each one is impressed with a certain phase of reality and emphasizes it over other phases. According to his view, every system has some degree of truth in it.

92) p. 244 Ferdinand C. S. Schiller (1864-1937) said man is a doer rather than a knower; his practical interests come first. Moral and

religious concerns play a fundamental part in what man believes is true, as knowledge. All that man ever succeeds in reaching is opinion.

93) p. 246 George Santayana (1863-1952) [Harvard, Rome] asserted the operation of the universe is mechanical and is unaffected by mind, the function of which is purely contemplative. The fundamental character of the universe is neither moral nor rational. He contended that mind itself is a product of matter in motion; under certain conditions, it becomes conscious of itself. It develops likes and dislikes, which are the root of value—goodness, beauty, imagination. He was convinced that a fundamental error of philosophy and religion lies in their confusing ideals with existences. Truth, goodness, and beauty are the real divinities, independent of each other, and often hostile, though the function of reason is to affect as great a harmony as possible. [The universe is not moral.]

94) p. 265 Ludwig Wittgenstein (1889-1951) [Cambridge]. A considerable portion of philosophy represents an attempt to state what can only be shown, and, therefore, it results in meaningless efforts to say the "unsayable."

95) p. 282 Lewis Mumford (1895-1990) [Dartmouth]. His basic question was: What shall the modern man do to be saved? The future of man is at stake and must be assured by a militant democracy, which maintains its responsibility for the sacredness of human life. This constitutes the challenge to education, a call for the development of new devotion to the whole of human society. It is a further challenge to a renewal of proper orientation to life that will transform men by carrying them beyond their ambiguous moral conceptions to a higher fulfillment of the meaning of life, giving it significance in the light of its place in the total cosmos. [This indicates to me the importance of everyone knowing UC.]

96) p. 292 Paul Tillich (1886-1965) [Berlin, Harvard] treated the question of reason and revelation, interpreting the latter in a broad sense as concerned not merely with what is beyond reason, but as any process of making Truth evident. The Being of God becomes the identity of "Being" and "God." God is personal, and as every person is self-transcendent, is not beyond the universe, nor merely within it,

but within it yet infinitely transcending it. The significance of Christ and the church is found in the new Being that one gains in the life of the church.

APPENDIX 9
POSTSCRIPT

I LAUGH TO MYSELF AND ULTIMATE CAUSE
THE GREAT DRAMA

In Ultimate Cause, religions are united in one community. In Ultimate Cause, religions, philosophies, and sciences are united.

The greatest thought I know is to think about Ultimate Cause. The most elegant logic is to know Ultimate Cause.

****

I smile to myself whenever I talk (think) to C. It is so wonderful and so absurd to think I am talking to the cause of the whole universe of astronomy, physics, humanity. But I know I have the full attention of C. C is capable of giving full attention to everyone.

"Well, C. (I seem to always start out thinking to C with 'well'. It indicates we are thinking about what has transpired.) Here I am, alive, mortal, thinking to you. I am alive and won't be for long. But I am now, as my father and mother were, and all the people of the past. What you have beyond this life for us, I have no idea beyond remembering us. But from my experience on earth, I know it is all right."

When I think of my not being here, in the not-distant future, I grin, smile, laugh to myself. It amuses me to think of my not being here experiencing with C, as we have been. But C will continue to experience this earth, the people, the whole universe as C did before I was here. It comforts me to think of C, my companion, experiencing when I am no longer here what we experienced together now. It is a pleasant thought, thinking into the future.

****

To know ourselves, to share the experiences of other people, to experience another person, is to experience somewhat as Ultimate Cause. It fulfills the longing of being. It makes life full. To know and experience with Ultimate Cause is complete fulfillment of life.

PRESENCE

Ultimate Cause is present everywhere.
Presence is being aware and being known.
Ultimate Cause is aware and is known.

We are in the presence of Ultimate Cause.
We are aware of Ultimate Cause.
Presence is being aware and being an influence.
UC being known is an influence.

Ultimate Cause is present everywhere.
We are in the presence of Ultimate Cause.
Ultimate Cause is aware of us.
Ultimate Cause knows us.
We know Ultimate Cause.

WHY SEE THE UNIVERSE AS A DRAMA

Ultimate Cause made the universe processes of development. The development has gone through galaxies to the earth and us. It includes our development from living by instinct to rational living. We see all the carnage in the world, natural disasters, predators and prey, inhumanity of man to man. We know Ultimate Cause made it so it developed to be as it is. The only explanation that makes sense is that it is a drama for Ultimate Cause.

Morality is our problem. The drama is our developing from instinctive living to rational living. Each of us makes our contribution to the development of rational living and C's experience.

The universe is capable of being aware of itself.
We are the universe aware of itself and its cause.
(Santayana --Philosopher 93)

I laugh as I talk to C. (It is so seemingly absurd and wonderful.) C knows my thoughts better than I do.

"Well, C, I won't be here long. I have written about you. I have told people how they can think of you. As time goes on, more and more people will. It has been a joy, a pleasure beyond compare. Thanks, UC."

I have shared my thoughts about cause of the universe.

You know Ultimate Cause.

APPENDIX 10
THOUGHTS

The universe is such that under certain circumstances, it can be aware of itself. We are that circumstance. We are the universe aware of itself and its cause.

I am as convinced that Ultimate Cause of the universe is my companion as I am that I am. I laugh to UC about the mortality drama we play. You too may know UC, if it be given you.

You will know you are beginning to think in terms of Ultimate Cause when you stand in front of the mirror, before you have dressed, (especially when you are over eighty) and laugh to UC, saying something like, "Well, UC, you caused it so it would develop to be this way." And you think UC's answer from your knowledge of the universe, "Yeah. It is a great show, isn't it. You would think it a great show if you had made it, wouldn't you?" You agree, as you think about the many people and cultures of the earth.

[The same is true when you are eight, twelve, eighteen, and twenty-two, and look at your beauty.]

The big problem facing mankind is how to structure society so everyone has a place in society to contribute to the economy and receive services for living a comfortable life. Otherwise we continue conflict in competitive society.

****

Looking around, I say to Ultimate Cause, "UC, you are the final cause back of all I see: the people, the trees, the grass, the dogs, the birds, the lakes, the rivers, the oceans. UC, you are the first cause, cause of causes. You are the ultimate cause of all we know from astronomy, physics, chemistry, biology, anthropology. You are cause of it all. It is all processes. It is all mortal. It is just as you want it. You are enjoying it all. It is a great drama.

"I think of you enjoying it with me and through me. You are my companion. I like to think of you enjoying it when I am no longer here, as you enjoyed it before I came. I like to think of my whole life of thoughts, feelings, words, and deeds in your memory beyond the existence of the universe."

When all is said and done, memories remain. In Ultimate Cause, our whole lives are like virtual realities beyond the existence of the universe. Our recording devices are examples of memory that enable us to think of UC.

When I am in pain, hurting, and when I look in the mirror, seeing the deterioration of age, I laugh and say to Ultimate Cause, "UC, you made it to be this way. It is a drama for you to enjoy. I am enjoying it too. It is a privilege to be part of your drama. Thank you for the processes that result in me being self-aware."

Do you say the same things to God? Do you think of God in the same way? If you want a logical understanding, then you either redefine God as Ultimate Cause or you think of UC directly.

Does one laugh to God that is moral and considers us sinners?

We laugh to UC about our situation because we know UC is experiencing our every thought and feeling with us, likes and enjoys us unconditionally. It is funny and seemingly absurd that in our mortality we know the cause and purpose of our being.

MEMORIES

I am thinking of those who have made my life: family, friends, companions on the road of life. Some are close friends, some brief acquaintances. Many have passed on. I think of each one in situations. Multitudes of them keep coming into my mind. You are in my memory.

We enjoy thinking back over experiences. We make new experiences. We make new friends. I think of you reading about Ultimate Cause. I think of you whom I have not met, reading about Ultimate Cause.

What a wonderful life I have had. You have made it. It is complete with ticks of laughter, self-expression in jokes missteps that make for tension and then understanding, exploring life together, sharing our thoughts and feelings.

Thank you, friends. Thank you who have passed on. Thank you who are still in the experience of the earth. We may still interact as part of the drama for Ultimate Cause.

I wish this book had been available to those who can no longer read and know Ultimate Cause as their companion. I make it available as soon as I can. It has taken more than seventy years.

I am not satisfied being part of the mortal universe. I want to be part of that which is beyond the universe. Ultimate Cause does this. We are all in the memory of UC beyond the universe. Perhaps we are more than in UC's memory. Everything depends on Ultimate Cause of the whole universe.

PURPOSE

The purpose of this book is to provide the resources to think of Ultimate Cause as your companion and have the point of view of UC.

REPETITION IS PRACTICE

Repetition increase familiarity. When you know UC is your companion, you will be comfortable with the repetitions and even welcome them. Repetition is practice, thinking about UC. Reading this book once may not be enough for the idea of UC to be part of your every day thought. UC means more and more to me after thinking about UC for seventy years.

NOTICE

Lewis Mumford advocated orientating life beyond ambiguous moral conceptions to a higher meaning of life. He saw the need to make life significant in the total cosmos.

This is exactly what knowing Ultimate Cause does. The highest meaning of life is realized when we know Ultimate Cause is experiencing our unique lives with us. We are significant beyond the cosmos in that the whole of our lives are in UC's memory beyond the existence of the universe.

For mankind to have peace, goodwill, and prosperity, all people need to think in terms of Ultimate Cause. Ultimate Cause is our companion. UC knows our every thought and feeling. We are united with all other people in that UC is our companion. We feel our responsibility for morality as we experience together.

The lasting importance of our lives is that UC is our companion. What can be greater than having UC as our companion? We enjoy everyone as UC does. We feel united with all the people of the earth in that we have UC as our mutual companion. Our place in the cosmos is that we are UC's companions. We experience the great drama of the universe with UC. The whole of our lives is preserved in UC's memory outside the universe.

From the beginning of human thought people have tried and done the best they could to know Ultimate Cause. People have tried many ideas that have been classified under the word "God." We are privileged to have information and perspective to know cause of the universe.

This is a how-to book. It tells why we need to think about cause of the universe. It provides resources. It tells how to think about Ultimate Cause and gives examples. I hope it is enough, so you enjoy thinking about UC.

The capstone of a full life is to know Ultimate Cause of the universe is your companion. Fulfillment of life is knowing another and know you are known by another. You know UC and know you are known by UC.

UC is capable of experiencing every thought and feeling of every moment of our lives, including our state of mind and circumstances of the moment, including the background of our whole lives.

THINK OUTSIDE THE BOX

The universe is a box.
Think outside the box.
Think of cause of the box.
Thought envelops the box.
That is Ultimate Cause.
UC envelops the universe.
UC is aware of everything.

The box is mortal. It disappears.
UC remains. I am in UC.
We are all in UC's memory.

We are the universe aware of itself and its cause.

CAN WE AGREE

Can we agree that there is cause of the universe?

Can we agree there is Ultimate Cause, for which we can use any symbol, using C and UC for now?

Can we agree that we can know UC by inference from our knowledge of the universe?

Can we agree we can know UC in human terms?

Can we agree that UC is capable of causing the universe to be as it is, as UC wants it without opposition?

Can we agree that UC is capable of knowing all about what happens and remembering it all?

Can we agree that UC caused the universe to enjoy it? We know of no reason UC would need the universe.

Can we agree that UC caused the universe to be processes and recycling? So, morality and ethics are our problem.

Can we agree there are many ideas of God, or many gods (for a person's idea of God is God to that person)?

Can we agree that to avoid confusing UC with being just another God (or idea of God) we use the designation Ultimate Cause?

Can we agree that since UC caused the universe to be as UC wanted it (without opposition), UC does not judge, and remembers everyone beyond the universe?

Can we agree that since UC knows our every thought and feeling, we can communicate with UC by our thoughts and we can think UC's response from our knowledge of the universe?

WHY THINK OF ULTIMATE CAUSE?

Why should you take time and effort to think of and promote the idea of UC? Because: your future, the future of your descendants and the future of mankind depend on you and other people who base their thinking on UC. Thinking about UC brings personal tranquility and social harmony. It encourages the development of infrastructures that provide adequately for every person on earth (one of whom you are). It encourages all people to be moral for the sake of humanity and themselves. Because you see the difference where the idea of UC is a strong influence, compared to where there is no idea of UC or the ideas of God dominates to a theistic state.

Ultimate Cause being known by inference from our knowledge of the universe cannot be God of a theistic state, because God of a theistic state giving guidance, would be inferring from a completely inferred cause, We cannot infer anything about the universe from our knowledge of UC. So those who know UC cannot claim to have instructions from UC. UC cannot be an active God.

Where the idea of God is the prevailing influence, the government is based on the irrefutable message of God. God's message was given to special people, is interpreted by clerics, enforced by social controls and government power. God is moral. God favors people who believe in him and handicaps non-believers. The government serves God and people who believe in that idea of God. People submit, are driven out, or there is constant tension and conflict.

Where the idea of cause of the universe is the prevailing influence, the government is based on the equality of man. Equal rights are written into the law by legislatures, and enforced by the courts. The goal is peace, prosperity, social harmony, and public safety. The rights of people to life, liberty, and the pursuit of happiness are maintained. The four freedoms: freedom of speech, of religion, from fear, and from want are respected and fostered.

It makes a difference to you yourself and to all mankind what you believe about Ultimate Cause, God and the gods. What you believe influences your thinking, what you do and support, the government, social structures and moral standards of the community and nation in which you live, which affects all the people of the world.

You may ignore cause of the universe. You may forget about Ultimate Cause. They are not going away.

****

WRITE YOUR OWN DIARY OF THOUGHTS ABOUT ULTIMATE CAUSE.

BIBLIOGRAPHY

1.
Calvin, John, (1509-1564) *Institutes of the Christian Religion* by John Calvin, translated from the Latin and Collated with the author's last edition in French by John Allen, in two volumes, Presbyterian Board of Christian Education, 1936.

2.
Calvin, John, *A Compend of the Institutes of the Christian Religion by John Calvin,* Edited by Hugh Thompson Kerr Jr., Presbyterian Board of Christian Education, 1939.

3.
Davis, John D, *A Dictionary of the Bible* by John D. Davis, Third Edition, The Westminster Press, Philadelphia 1920.

4.
ENCYCLOPEDIA BRITANNICA, William Benton, Publisher. Chicago: London: Toronto. 1959, 24 Volumes.

5.
Funk & Wagnalls Standard Dictionary of the English Language International Edition Combined with Britannica World Language Dictionary, Two Volumes. Encyclopedia Britannica, Inc, Chicago Funk & Wagnalls Company, New York, 1958.

6.
Handbook in the History of Philosophy 3500 BC to the Present by Albert E. Avey, Barns and Noble College Outline Series, no. 90, Second Edition, Copyright, 1954, 1961, Reprinted 1969, Barns and Noble, Inc, New York.

7.
Hoyt's, *New Cyclopedia of Practical Quotations*, Compiled by Kate Louise Roberts, Funk & Wagnalls Company, New York and London, 1940.

8.

Luther, Martin, *A Compend of Luther's Theology*, Edited by Hugh Thomson Kerr Jr., The Westminster Press, Philadelphia, (1943).

9.

Modern Philosophy: An Anthology of Primary Sources. Edited by Roger, Ariew, Hackett Publishing Company, Inc. Indianapolis, Cambridge 1998.

10.

The Interlinear Bible, Hebrew, Greek, English, Jay P. Green Sr. General Editor and Translator: Baker Book House Company, Grand Rapids, Michigan 49506, 1981.

11.

The New Webster Encyclopedic Dictionary of the English Language Including A Dictionary of Synonyms and Twelve Supplementary Reference Sections, Virginia S. Thatcher Editor in Chief Alexander McQueen Advisory Editor and Lexicographer, Published by Consolidated Book Publishers, Chicago, MCMLII.

12.

The Westminster Confession of Faith in The Constitution of the Presbyterian Church (U.S.A.) Part I Book of Confessions, Published by the Office of the General Assembly, 100 Witherspoon Street, Louisville. KY 40202-1396, 1991.

13.

The Qur'an, Translation, by M.H. Shakir, Published by, Tahrike Tarsile Qur'an, Inc. Published and Distributors of Holy Qur'an 80-08 51st Avenue, Elmhurst, New York 11373.

You may e-mail me with comments (expect no response) at: ultimate_cause@yahoo.com

Purchase at: 1-888-280-7715, bkorders@authorhouse.com

Printed in the United States
34707LVS00005B/76-222